Praise for *Not Even a Grain of Rice: Buying Food on Credit in the Dominican Republic*

"Christine Hippert's beautifully written book uses vivid ethnographic detail to address poverty, class, gender, race, and racism in the Dominican Republic. Focusing on food shopping in the small stores called *colmados*, it reveals the navigation of relations between Haitians and Dominicans based on the extension of credit called *fiao*. Their highly complex relations go beyond race and depend on assessments of people's responsibility in paying debts and helping others. This fascinating book contributes to food studies, the anthropology of race, and Caribbean studies."

—**Carole Counihan**, editor-in-chief, *Food and Foodways*

"Grounded in rich ethnographic engagement, Hippert reveals the complexities of race and social hierarchies in the context of international tourists and Haitians living and working in the Dominican Republic. By focusing on local forms of support and mutual aid around food access, *Not Even a Grain of Rice* upends our understanding of race relations in the Dominican Republic, revealing the ways that community members support one another across difference."

—**Hanna Garth**, University of California,
San Diego; author of *Food in Cuba: The Pursuit of a Decent Meal*

"*Not Even a Grain of Rice* is a fine-grained and compassionate ethnography of the social networks and structures of trust forged through microloans within corner groceries or *colmados* in Cabarete, Dominican Republic. This study reveals how Dominicans and Haitians are entangled in webs of reciprocity that remain unseen in studies that focus only on speech acts, offering an invaluable corrective to a literature that all too often focuses on urban elite discourse. This compelling and important study deserves a wide readership among those interested in Haiti, the Dominican Republic, and the Caribbean more generally, as well as issues of food insecurity among the working poor."

—**Lauren Derby**, University of California, Los Angeles;
co-editor of *The Dominican Republic Reader*

"*Not Even a Grain of Rice* disentangles race and racism, identity, and practices of reciprocity on the fraught, divided island of Hispaniola. Digging beneath the official anti-Haitianism, Hippert's rich ethnography of a Dominican town portrays a nuanced, complex understanding of everyday people's beliefs and practices, which don't always align."

—**Mark Schuller**, Northern Illinois University; author of
Humanity's Last Stand: Confronting Global Catastrophe

"*Not Even a Grain of Rice* is a beautifully written and ethnographically rich account of life in Cabarete, Dominican Republic, on the north coast. Hippert offers a refreshing view of relationships that emerge over time between Dominicans and Haitians in the coastal community in the neighborhood *colmado*. The *colmado* becomes an important cultural symbol of different interactions and transactions where people often shop with store credit (*fiao*) and build social relationships and community. While *Not Even a Grain of Rice* brings into focus the effects of food insecurity, social inequality, and the practices of *fiao*, the stories throughout the book shed light on the shared humanity in the community built on trust and social relationships."

—**Kimberly Eison Simmons**, University of South Carolina,
author of *Reconstructing Racial Identity and the African
Past in the Dominican Republic*

"Hippert's *Not Even a Grain of Rice* is a food-related ethnography that shows the precarious relationships that develop to access food based on one's word as a currency and as a social glue to express social and economic solidarity in the Dominican Republic. This work is timely in addressing how people navigate their race, class, and gender in the wider realms of anti-Blackness where privilege and exclusion truncate the trust built on people's commitment to buy now and pay later. Throughout the Americas, shop owners have signs that read "hoy no fio y mañana tampoco," warning consumers their word is just not enough to honor the social contracts that have built community and have kept people alive for generations. This book makes a wonderful contribution to the scholarship on food insecurity, food sovereignty, and the ethnography of everyday life and making do in the Caribbean."

—**Guillermina Gina Nunez-Mchiri**, University of Texas at El Paso

"With rich ethnographic granularity and sensitivity to the everyday experiences and intercultural tensions that characterize neighborhood life for so many in today's Dominic Republic, Hippert clearly and convincingly shows how matters of race, nationality, subsistence, privilege, and morality all intersect and find expression in the simple act of food shopping at local colmados (corner stores). Before I even finished reading *Not Even a Grain of Rice*, I knew that I would be assigning it in my classes."

—**Ty Matejowsky**, University of Central Florida,
author of *Fast Food Globalization in the Provincial Philippines*

"*Not Even a Grain of Rice* offers readers an in-depth, nuanced perspective about the intricacies of intersectionality and its connection to food, space, and place. Hippert's work makes seemingly ordinary, invisible aspects of everyday life visible through the examination of intercultural relationships between Dominicans, Haitians, and Dominico-Haitians throughout their interactions at colmados. By interweaving countless examples of how these corner stores function as anchors within daily life, this book interrogates simplistic notions about race, class, gender, economics, and politics by expanding our understanding of their meanings. It makes a stellar contribution, both to and beyond the field of food studies."

—**Carlnita P. Greene**, Bunker Hill Community College, author of
Gourmands & Gluttons: The Rhetoric of Food Excess

"Hippert's eloquent storytelling nuanced through rich field notes broadens understandings of food security to include webs of social processes and power involved in buying groceries through the *fiao* credit system in the tourist town of Cabarate, Dominican Republic. Hippert's illuminating work aptly pushes the boundaries of food studies by using everyday transactions and interactions in *colmados* to surface a complicated history of race, class, gender, and citizenship for working-class Haitians and Dominicans."

—**Sarah Fouts**, University of Maryland, Baltimore County

"*Not Even a Grain of Rice* brings together a considerable amount of empirical data on the important place of *colmados*—ubiquitous corner stores—in the provisioning strategies of poor and working-class Dominicans in Cabarete, Dominican Republic. Situated at the crossroads of migrant labor, tourism, and plural ethnic communities, Hippert's study sheds light on the microeconomic exchanges that sustain a system of mutual aid between shopkeepers and patrons. Through detailed vignettes, readers are introduced to the quotidian negotiations of in-store credit acquisition, borrowing, and debt—and the moral entanglements these activities inspire—that are central to the enduring viability and cultural significance of these essential grocers at the local level. A welcome contribution to ethnographic studies of food shopping and the microeconomics of household sustainability."

—**Brendan Jamal Thornton**, University of North Carolina at
Chapel Hill; author of *Negotiating Respect: Pentecostalism, Masculinity,
and the Politics of Spiritual Authority in the Dominican Republic*

"*Not Even a Grain of Rice* is an important contribution to various fields, including Dominican studies, Caribbean studies, food studies, and Haitian studies. Hippert offers a thoughtful and imminently readable account of how a common practice in the Dominican Republic—*comprando fiao*, or buying food on credit from small neighborhood *colmados* (stores)—offers a window into the relationships between Dominicans, Dominicans of Haitian Descent, and Haitian (im)migrants in the northern coastal town of Cabarete, a popular ecotourism destination. Hippert argues that the commonplace anti-Haitianist rhetoric, discourses, and beliefs espoused by many Dominicans and their government alike should not be taken at face value. Instead, the equally salient social fact of class-based solidarity between and among the multiethnic residents of La Cienaga and Callejón de la Loma is evidenced in the moral economy of the *fiao* (informal credit) system. Simply stated, despite the surge in and institutionalization of contemporary anti-Haitian rhetoric and practices, Dominican *colmaderos* routinely label Haitians and Dominicans of Haitian descent *gente responsable* (responsible people)—a racialized assessment of trustworthiness upon which the ability to purchase the food necessary for survival hinges. As Hippert ably argues, this case exemplifies the coexistence of anti-Haitian discourses and everyday Dominco-Haitian solidarity practices."

—**Ginetta E.B. Candelario**, Smith College; author of *Black behind the Ears:
Dominican Racial Identity from Museums to Beauty Shops*

Not Even a Grain of Rice

CROSSING BORDERS IN A GLOBAL WORLD: APPLYING ANTHROPOLOGY TO MIGRATION, DISPLACEMENT, AND SOCIAL CHANGE

Series Editors: Raúl Sánchez Molina (ersanchez@fsof.uned.es) and Nancy Anne Konvalinka (nkonvalinka@fsof.uned.es)

Mission Statement

By crossing political, social, cultural, and identity borders current migrants, refugees, and travelers meet challenges of globalization in their processes of displacement, incorporation, and adaptation to new settlements. These circumstances open up opportunities for anthropologists and members of related disciplines to work together with migrants, residents, and communities seeking to contribute to knowledge and action. This series seeks to address these challenges and their intersections with national, ethnic, gender, and generational identities by providing a range of interdisciplinary theoretical and methodological frameworks of how scholars and practitioners can approach not only knowledge, but also application. In addition, this series aims to show models of collaboration and interaction in economy, policy, social and physical reproduction, health, labor market, education, and other social institutions. In doing so, the series should be of value to scholars studying historical and contemporary issues in displacement, migration, immigration, and development studies as well as advanced undergraduate and graduate students and practitioners interested in the impact of displacements, migration, and social and cultural changes in contemporary societies. Some examples of specific movements are migrants from less to more affluent areas, migrants escaping violence in their home contexts, migrants sent abroad by their companies, and people seeking medical and reproductive treatments unavailable at home.

Advisory Board

Maria Eugenia Bozzoli, Adi Bharadwaj, Monica Bonaccorso, Lucy M. Cohen, Yasmine Ergas, Andrés Fábregas Puig, Carles Feixa, Ubaldo Martínez Veiga, Marit Melhuus, Alicia Re Cruz, Amy Speier, Meenakshi Thapan, and María Amelia Viteri

Books in Series

Not Even a Grain of Rice: Buying Food on Credit in the Dominican Republic, by Christine Hippert
Resettling Displaced Communities: Applying the International Standard for Involuntary Resettlement, by William L. Partridge and David B. Halmo
Identities on Trial in the United States: Asylum Seekers from Asia, by ChorSwang Ngin
The Crux of Refugee Resettlement: Rebuilding Social Networks, edited by Andrew Nelson, Alexander Rödlach, and Roos Willems

Not Even a Grain of Rice

Buying Food on Credit in the Dominican Republic

Christine Hippert

LEXINGTON BOOKS
Lanham • Boulder • New York • London

Published by Lexington Books
An imprint of The Rowman & Littlefield Publishing Group, Inc.
4501 Forbes Boulevard, Suite 200, Lanham, Maryland 20706
www.rowman.com

6 Tinworth Street, London SE11 5AL, United Kingdom

British Library Cataloguing in Publication Information Available

Library of Congress Control Number: 2020947186

ISBN: 978-1-4985-6960-6 (cloth)
ISBN: 978-1-4985-6962-0 (pbk)
ISBN: 978-1-4985-6961-3 (electronic)

Contents

List of Figures and Table

LIST OF FIGURES

LIST OF TABLE

Preface

Not Even a Grain of Rice, first and foremost, tells the story of people building relationships with others through food. But this is also a story of power, privilege, and the social constructions of race and racism. My research shows that in the context of food shopping in small corner stores in Cabarete, an important international destination in the Dominican Republic, working-class residents harbor racial prejudice while simultaneously fostering a solidarity based upon class and, to a lesser extent, gender. The voices in this book express the complexity of what it means to invoke—or to have the power to invoke—privilege. These stories may be uniquely situated in the Dominican Republic, but the issues that are expressed are not singular to this place. Paying attention to people's experiences in this book can help shape our understanding of how class-based relationships mitigate anti-Black[1] racism in international, neoliberal, racist, and neocolonial contexts.

There are many manifestations of anti-Black racism around the world, including its murderous dimensions on display in the United States, my home country, at this moment. As I write this book, the United States is in the throes of a massive national-level reckoning—certainly not the first, but one that has gained momentum and appears to be truly historically significant. Contemporary events concerning the murder of Black people by the hands of law enforcement as well as the disparate experiences of white people and people of color during the current COVID-19 pandemic highlight the devastating economic, health, and safety implications of institutional racism. Breonna Taylor, George Floyd, and Rayshard Brooks are just three in a list of names of Black people who were killed or injured by police officers in the United States within the last few months. The disparity between people of color and white people in their experiences of COVID-19 is, in part, a product of the health insecurity that millions of Americans face in the United States because of our market-driven health-care system. Daily protests and everyday calls for social, racial, and economic justice abound in national news cycles. Meanwhile, undocumented people living and working in the United States express a very rational fear of the consequences they might face if they come out of the shadows to speak out against police brutality, systemic racism, or immigration policies that disparage them.

Writing a book on Haitian Dominican interpersonal relations in the Dominican Republic was, for me, a process that exposed my racial, national, and economic privilege throughout the entire research process. My research design involved the use of a variety of ethnographic methods, including living and working in the Dominican Republic, in which my own identity as a white, cisgender, financially secure, professional woman from the United States was considered and interpreted by people who did not share these identities. Additionally, my research elicited qualitative and quantitative data to understand the particularly delicate subjects of debt and hunger, subjects that people often feel uncomfortable discussing in polite company or with strangers. While many people opened up to me about their financial struggles in the context of relationships I developed with them, I had difficult conversations throughout my fieldwork as people sought to gauge my awareness of my own privilege and the history of unequal power relations between the United States and the Dominican Republic. For example, sometimes during the course of interviewing working-class residents in Cabarete, they would turn around and ask me about whether or not my sons had ever experienced hunger or if I had ever been unable to pay for food or was forced to skip meals— experiences that I had inquired of them as part of the interview process. They knew that my job as a college professor from the United States protected me and my family from the kind of food insecurity that they often experienced, but they asked me to see if I would shy away from talking about the inequality between our circumstances. Their questions gave me an opportunity, where possible, to deepen my relationships with those participants, and when I had complicated encounters that were more short-lived or superficial, I made sincere attempts to incorporate what I learned from these challenges in my approach to and analysis of the evidence.

Another story to illustrate my point: during a weekend respite from fieldwork, I attended a Xiomara Fortuna concert in Santo Domingo with some middle-class Dominican friends. During the evening, one of these friends told me, "I'm angry that you're even here," to which I asked for clarification. She replied, "Cristina, I can't travel like you do. I would love to go to the US, or Europe, or anyplace, but even though I have money to do so, it's very difficult for me to travel. I can't get a visa like you can." As a scholar from the United States, I filled out paperwork on the plane and paid a US$10 fee at the airport in Santo Domingo for a visa to stay in the Dominican Republic, while acquiring a visa to live and work in the United States for Dominicans or Haitians requires a lengthy and more expensive process that begins months in advance and, in the end, is often rejected. This had been my friend's fate: she had tried and failed to garner a visa to travel internationally a few times, and she was frustrated by the ease with which I could travel to and stay in the Dominican Republic.

And one more example, highlighting my privilege: I was invited to present the results of my research to graduate students and faculty in the social sciences and humanities at the Universidad Autónoma de Santo Domingo (UASD). After my hour-long talk, a student's hand shot up, and when I called on her, she said she had five questions for me. But she prefaced these questions by exclaiming, "I have a sister in your country who has been trying to regularize her status for 9 years and has been unable to do so." It made this student angry that my research interrogated historical racism and anti-Haitianism in the Dominican Republic while these same types of problems have persisted and continue to persist in the United States. In my response to her, I acknowledged her comment and validated her frustration. The inequalities in my own country involving racism and xenophobia are abhorrent and must be changed. But I'm certain that some of my comments were not all that comforting to her: I'm critical of institutionalized racism and xenophobia in both the United States and the Dominican Republic, and I'm also critical of my own place within systems of oppression in both contexts. After she finished with her questions, another student told everyone in attendance that the Dominican Republic is not a racist country, to which one Haitian and many other Dominican students responded by saying that he was wrong: they themselves had indeed witnessed and experienced racism in their own country.

Sitting with and reflecting on these uncomfortable exchanges is a necessary first step in the process of engaging in the work of anti-racism. I offer the above stories of people's astute observations and comments to stress the relevance of multiple dimensions of inequality. Bonilla-Silva (2014, 15) argues for a move away from "being nonracist to becoming antiracist":

> Being an antiracist begins with understanding the institutional nature of racial matters and accepting that all actors in a racialized society are affected *materially* (receive benefits or disadvantages) and *ideologically* by the racial structure. This stand implies taking responsibility for your unwilling participation in these practices and beginning a new life committed to the goal of achieving real racial equality.

The conversation I engaged in during my UASD presentation is similar to other conversations I have had about the complex meanings of institutional racism in the United States. It also centered the history of U.S. imperialism in the Dominican Republic, as well as the hostility Dominicans sometimes feel in the United States, especially when they are undocumented.

My research in the Dominican Republic stems from my scholarly interests in the ways that inequality is a product of social, historical, political, economic, and cultural processes in different places and times. In no way do I believe that the United States should be a model for others as we work to create policies and practices that dismantle systems of oppression. In writing this book, I wanted to illustrate the ways that racism is experienced by people of varying positionalities intersecting gender, class, and national origin to a varied audience of international scholars and students. My hope is that *Not Even a Grain of Rice* will help people in both the United States and the Dominican Republic recognize their own privilege in multiple and intersecting ways so that we can be willing and intentional participants in charting a way forward after centuries of injustice and entrenched inequality.

NOTE

1. Currently, there is an ongoing debate about the use of the word "Black" (with a capital -B) or "black" (e.g., Eligon 2020). This debate has been primarily situated in the context of the United States. In this book, I use black, with a lowercase -b, to discuss the social constructions of races and racism in the Dominican Republic, since that aligns with orthographic conventions in the literature on blackness in that context. But I use Black, with a capital -B, to distinguish the growing contemporary global movement working to raise awareness, restructure society, and rectify inequities within communities of color and between white people and people of color all over the world, such as the Black Lives Matter movement.

Acknowledgments

Ethnography is grounded in relationships, relationships built over a long period of time in different contexts. This book would not have been possible without the support from many people in both the United States and the Dominican Republic, some of those with whom I've worked since the beginning of this project in 2011. First, I want to extend my sincere appreciation to the residents of Cabarete, especially those who worked with me in the Callejón and La Cienaga. I have chosen to keep them anonymous in the book for several reasons, primarily out of concern for those who are living and working in the Dominican Republic without papers. But some of them have allowed me to acknowledge them without linking their names to other identifying stories or words: Dirogene, Sonia, Belkis, María, Oscar, Jaroni, Josué, Yanlesi, Rita, Ana, Jonny, Willy, Elizabeth, Bautista, Papitín, Jonás, Marisa, Tomás, Jean Michel, Ramona, Cesar, Wesmín, Anouse, Jherileidy, Miguelina, and Gustavo. To them, and to many others in Cabarete, thank you for your generosity, engagement, and contributions to my research, as well as to your genuine efforts to welcome me and my sons to life in Cabarete during our stay in the Dominican Republic.

The initial stage of this project was first encouraged by Natasha Musalém-Pérez when she was still a student at the University of Wisconsin-LaCrosse (UWL). Naty came to me in 2009 asking if I would be interested in developing a faculty-led study abroad program in the Dominican Republic. Her innocuous request and desire to "share her home country" with students in Wisconsin became a decade-long quest for me to interrogate and understand inequality, racism, and food security both in and between the Dominican Republic and the United States. Glenis Tavárez, at the Museo del Hombre in Santo Domingo, introduced me to Edwin Aristy Rosa, director of Las Raíces, a sustainable cultural tourism organization in Santo Domingo, who was pivotal in the implementation of my institution's first and only study abroad program in the Dominican Republic. My relationships with Edwin, his business partner Miguel Ángel Pérez Ortíz, and Lucyris Mateo were instrumental in helping me formulate my project and its location in Cabarete. For their institutional support, I want to thank the directing members of the Instituto Especializado de Estudios Superiores Loyola: Drs. Luciano Castillo Domínguez, John Henry Antonio Morales, and Lic. Jalinton Reyes Lemos. I also extend my sincere appreciation to Dra. Luisa Navarro, director of the Escuela de Historia y Antropología in the Facultad de Humanidades for extending an invitation to me to present some of my research results in March 2015 at the Universidad Autónoma de Santo Domingo. Bridget Wooding, coordinator at the Caribbean Migration and Development Observatory in Santo Domingo, interviewed with me and provided me with helpful resources. Finally, I am grateful to several residents of Cabarete who direct local NGOs, especially Patricia Suriel at the Mariposa Foundation for her friendship and advocacy for people living and working in Cabarete.

My research was generously supported by UWL by awarding me a year-long sabbatical in 2014–2015 and several faculty research and development grants to fund my research at various stages (during the summers of 2011, 2013, and 2014 as well as the academic year in 2014–2015). I'd like to thank my colleagues within the Department of Archaeology and Anthropology, especially the chair, Tim McAndrews, for awarding me a one-class teaching release to provide me more time to write. A warm word of thanks to Omar Granados, director of UWL's Institute for Latin American Studies, for our many conversations about food and cultural studies in the Caribbean, as well as for the opportunity to present my research during UWL's 2015 Hispanic Heritage Month celebration. Thank you to UWL's Writing Hunker program, which gave me the space and support to complete my book proposal, as well as to Laurie Cooper Stoll for her close reading of the proposal and her recommendation to submit the proposal to Lexington Press. I want to thank my students over the years for their feedback on my work, especially those in my Anthropology of Food, Search for Economic Justice, and Peoples and Cultures of Latin America classes. Thank you to Enilda Delgado for her careful reading of my sabbatical proposal, as well as for her thoughtful last-minute help as I prepared to travel to the Dominican Republic for the first time. My momentum to complete this project was sustained in no small part by Mahruq Khan, Keely Rees, and Sheryl Gora-Bollom. I want to single out Jodi Vandenberg-Daves, who I leaned on for advice and encouragement about a process that she had already completed. For all of her support and friendship, I am eternally grateful.

My work as an anthropologist and Latin American/Caribbean Studies scholar has been nurtured by a number of different mentors and colleagues to whom

I want to give credit here. To Rich Scaglion, thank you for being my "forever advisor." If I am half the model to junior faculty and students that you have been for me, then I have succeeded in learning the lessons you've taught me. Thank you, too, to Sarah Strauss and the late Carol McAllister, for their thoughtful and helpful advising during graduate school. To all of my colleagues in the North Central Council of Latin Americanists through the Center for Latin American and Caribbean Studies at the University of Wisconsin-Milwaukee, especially fellow members of the executive committee with whom I worked: Julie Kline, Elia Armacanqui-Tipacti, Eduardo Magalhães III, Mariano Magalhães, Margaret Crosby, Elena De Costa, Pedro A.G. dos Santos, Benjamín Narváez, and Shane Boeder, thank you for your friendship and your advocacy in Latin American and Caribbean Studies in the Upper Midwest. For their input on my work at the panel entitled, "'Hard Work' and 'Laziness' in Latin America: The Racial, Ethnic and Class Ideologies That Underpin Social Inequality," at the Latin American Studies Association 2019 congress in Boston, Massachusetts, I want to thank Miriam Shakow, William Girard, Abigail Adams, and Krista Van Vleet. At the Caribbean Studies Association meetings in 2019 in Santa Marta, Colombia, my fellow panelist, Dr. Charlene Roach, deputy dean in the Faculty of Social Sciences from the University of West Indies, provided me with a comparative context of in-store credit, referred to as trust, from other parts of the Caribbean. To explore this further, Charlene put me in touch with Marsha Winter and Aisha Baptiste for their library assistance at the University of West Indies, St. Augustine, Trinidad and Tobago. In the summer of 2012, I attended a five-day National Science Foundation methods workshop taught by Jeffrey Johnson and Christopher McCarty, and I want to thank them and the workshop attendees, especially Jennifer Jo Thompson, Gina Nuñez, Ty Matejowsky, and Mary Alice Scott, who provided invaluable feedback on my emerging project. I am grateful to Elena Guzmán and Daniela García-Grandon for their excellent work on Dominican-Haitian relations and Chilean in-store credit, respectively, and the collegiality they showed me in our correspondence. And for their editorial work on articles that have been published on my research, I want to thank Carole Counihan, Ken Irish-Bramble, and Carlnita Greene.

A special thanks to Kasey Beduhn, associate acquisitions editor at Lexington Press, for her patience and input on my work; to the editors of the series, *Crossing Borders in a Global World: Applying Anthropology to Migration, Displacement, and Social Change*, Raúl Sánchez Molina and Nancy Anne Konvalinka; and to the anonymous peer reviewer of my manuscript. All of their efforts improved the book. All remaining errors are my own responsibility.

Last, but certainly not least, I want to thank my family, to whom I dedicate this book. To my children, Eli and Jonah, who accompanied me in the Dominican Republic during my research: they give me hope in the wake of all of our current global uncertainty. And to my partner, Peter Stovall, who has seen and heard it all. I'm not sure if he knew what it meant to marry an anthropologist at the beginning of our relationship, but he certainly does now. He has been my rock, helping me keep perspective when I needed it. Thank you for all of your love and support.

Introduction

"Not Even a Grain of Rice"—Living and Working in a Precarious Place

11 July 2011

This morning I arrived at Wilman and Teresa's house around 9:00 to learn how to make a typical mid-day meal, the biggest meal of the day for both Dominicans and Haitians. This was the first time I had been invited to their home, a one room, tin-roofed shack, attached to the house of doña[1] Marisa and sandwiched between two very noisy neighbors. The whole neighborhood could hear the sounds of Romeo Santos, a Dominican-American bachata-star, echoing from the shack just a few meters away from Wilman and Teresa's front door. Teresa is a 24-year old Haitian migrant who had recently moved to this neighborhood in the Dominican Republic to live with her husband, Wilman, a gardener who has lived in the Dominican Republic since 2004. They had married in Haiti four years ago when Wilman was in Haiti visiting, but they decided to live apart because Teresa made some decent money working as a cook for her mother's small business run out of their home in southeastern Haiti. Teresa left Haiti in 2014 to join her husband in Cabarete only when she experienced health problems for which she received irregular and unsuccessful treatment in Haiti. She relocated to Cabarete with the help of friends and medical staff in Haiti and the Dominican Republic after having tumors removed from her uterus in a hospital in the Dominican city of Moca, about 60km away from Cabarete.

Teresa's kitchen area was a small, cramped corner of the main room of the house, consisting of: a few old plastic cement pails with interlocking lids in which she put rice; two book-shelves on the wall for storing a few mugs, glasses, plates, and a small empty yogurt container where she kept her silverware; and an oven range, which had a functioning stove top where she did her cooking. But Teresa used the non-functioning oven itself as a cupboard, a place to store spices and staple food items in small plastic bags such as white flour and salt. The last accoutrement in the kitchen was the requisite 5-gallon plastic container with a pumping mechanism to dispense potable water for cooking and drinking. Most Americans recognize these water containers as "water coolers," the kind that are turned upside down and placed in a mechanized unit that heats or cools the water when dispensed. The Dominican Republic does not have the funds necessary to treat their water in a public health facility, so most residents use water containers with a hand pump like this one for all of their water needs even if they have sinks in their kitchens, something that was absent from Wilman and Teresa's home.

Teresa and Wilman's bed was just a few feet away from the kitchen area, and cordoned off from the rest of their home with an old bed sheet draped from the ceiling. Across from the bed area was a 3 × 5 foot dry-walled cubicle containing a flush toilet and a spigot coming out of the wall used for bathing. This area was very cramped; if the spigot was turned on, the water spilled out onto the toilet. There was a large empty plastic tub filled with water from the spigot to use for hand-washing. The dimensions of the entire home were only 15 × 18 feet, so there was very little room for us to sit inside on the deteriorating plastic chairs that she offered me upon my arrival. We moved out onto the cement block that they called the patio in front of the front door to work on preparations for the mid-day meal. When I arrived at Teresa's house, she was hard at work shelling guandules (Dominican Spanish for pigeon peas) from their husks, and de-feathering a dead chicken, the very one that we would cook that morning for the mid-day meal. For the next hour and a half, I helped Teresa wash, peel, and cut vegetables, boil rice, and prepare the chicken that had only been butchered an hour ago at the corner store where she purchased it. Usually, customers buy meat already gutted and de-feathered, but Teresa saved some money this morning by doing that work herself, especially when she knew I was coming to help her.

At 10:45 am, Teresa looked at me wide-eyed and gasped, and we engaged in the ensuing conversation:

"Oh no, I forgot chicken bouillon for the sauce. Oh, help me Lord, I hope I can buy it," exclaimed Teresa.

"Do you have any money?" I asked. "Let's head over to Pepe's corner store right now and we'll have it in time to add it to the sauce."

"No, I never have any money. But Ricardo isn't working this month, and I never work," she replied.

I looked at her, confused, and cautiously offered, "Then I can lend you the money. We're cooking for all of us, so of course I can contribute, too."

"But Cristina, for the past two days, I've eaten not even a single grain of rice. I can't go to Pepe's and Ana's corner stores, because I've gone there too often. If you lend me the money, they'll make you pay for everything, you know?"

I decidedly did not know; frankly, I had absolutely no idea what she was talking about. Her comments left me with so many questions. What did she mean by, "they'll make you pay for everything?" Hadn't I offered to pay for the chicken bouillon? What else would I need to pay for? Why had she brought up Ricardo, her husband's friend, and what was the relevance of his job as an on-again/off-again construction worker? Did she typically borrow money from Ricardo to buy food, and now she felt stuck because he "wasn't working this month?" And why would the corner store owners she referred to, Pepe and Ana, be concerned with her returning to their stores "too often" to buy food? Many stores in which I had shopped looked like they could have used a few more paying customers: several of their shelves and food bins were empty, and customers who had come to rely on a particular shop for certain food items were turned away by shopkeepers who weren't able to upkeep their stock. Don't shopkeepers want loyal, returning customers? But I had shopped at Pepe's store many times; his corner store wasn't one of the ones in which I observed nearly bare shelves. In fact, Pepe's corner store looked to be doing economically well: he often had lines of customers out the door during the late morning when women, who had been cooking the midday meal and noticed that they had run out of a certain staple, sent their children on the errand of purchasing a small amount of whatever was needed at the moment.

Or, conversely, did Teresa mean that sparse shelves in corner stores meant that stores' supplies couldn't keep up with customers' demand? That, maybe, Teresa was reluctant to go to Pepe's and Ana's stores because she wouldn't find what she was looking for, and she was worried about not preparing the midday meal in time for her husband, Wilman, who would expect to eat his meal quickly and then rush off to his next job? And why did Teresa say that she hadn't even eaten "a single grain of rice" for the past two days? I had eaten with her at my home just the day before. Together, we had prepared and eaten a lunch consisting of rice, bean sauce, stewed eggplant, carrots, potatoes, and chicken in a bouillon sauce, typical creole food (*comida criolla* in Spanish and *manje kreyòl* in Kreyòl, the national language of Haiti). Therefore, I had evidence to the contrary about her exclamation that she had gone without rice. I wondered if she had just forgotten what we had cooked together, or if not eating a single grain of rice had some other symbolic meaning, one that I hadn't encountered yet in my research.

The conversation above between Teresa and me took place at the very beginning of my research in the Dominican Republic. Prior to my conversation with Teresa, I had heard similar sentiments from two different people: one person told me that they had to avoid one corner store because the owner thought he wasn't "responsible," and the other person had informed me that she only shopped at a particular corner store because she ran up a tab—the first of many references I had heard made about shopping on a tab, or buying food using in-store credit, what residents called *fiao* in Spanish. What followed was a multiyear ethnographic study to gain a better understanding of how food shopping practices were structured to help or hurt people's chances of eating on any given day.

Not Even a Grain of Rice: Buying Food on Credit in the Dominican Republic is an ethnography of food shopping in corner stores and the significance of fiao in the development of social relationships between working-class Haitians and Dominicans living and working in the tourist industry along the north coast of the Dominican Republic. There is a strong economic incentive to offer in-store credit to buy food to stave off financial insecurity and hunger, creating networks of intercultural solidarity. Over time, a moral economy has emerged within corner stores based upon perceptions of class, gender, and a shared sense of dignity through credit, even while racism and discrimination persist among the same population.

The goals of this book are twofold: (1) to examine the ways that poor communities in neocolonial settings, particularly multicultural communities that are magnets for migrant labor, provision their households, and (2) to illustrate people's experiences of race and racism in a global context. To shed light on the ways migrants and nonmigrants create and maintain their lives in an intercultural community, the book examines the intersecting relationships among three pivotal variables: (1) the challenges people face as they move within, to, and from the Dominican Republic to make a living, (2) the way people maintain and re-create social groups, and (3) the survival strategies that people use to provision their households. Analyzing these variables in context problematizes the "natural" internal logic of inclusion/exclusion and challenges our assumptions of what it means to live and work in a transnational world. People's experiences with food shopping, debt, and survival reveal a more complicated interpersonal engagement between Haitians and Dominicans than has been previously assumed, both in the scholarly literature as well as in colloquial presumptions of everyday intercultural relations between Dominicans and Haitians.

Yet buying food using in-store credit fails to minimize economic inequality for residents of the Callejón and La Cienaga, two working-class neighborhoods in Cabarete where those who comprise the bottom echelon of the tourism industry reside. Tourism is one of the most economically viable industries in the Dominican Republic, which has attracted low-income migrant laborers as well as tourists or part-time residents (often known as "snowbirds") from around the world. For several decades, anthropological studies of tourism have emphasized the irregular effects of tourism on people all over the world, such as whether people are able to exert agency to maintain or modify cultural practices in the wake of exchanges between hosts and guests (e.g.,

Smith 1989). Additionally, anthropologists have been critical of the capacity of tourism to promote economic development (Di Giovine 2018). *Not Even a Grain of Rice* questions the role of fiao in alleviating poverty as well as its place in people's emerging conceptions of morality in this neoliberal, international tourism destination.

ANTI-HAITIANISM AND THE LEGACIES OF THE PAST IN THE PRESENT

In the Dominican Republic, race has become synonymous with conceptions of citizenship: who belongs and who gets to belong, given the long history of border relations between Haiti and the Dominican Republic (García-Peña 2016; Moya Pons 1998). The history of the social construction of races in the Dominican Republic has been a complex process shaped by colonialism and the slave trade. In my anthropology classes, this process is often difficult for students to grasp because to people who have grown up in the United States, most Haitians and most Dominicans would find themselves categorized into the same racial group: people of African descent. But the social hierarchy of races in the Dominican Republic spans the color spectrum, of varying shades of white to black, in a way that is fundamentally different from the social construction of race in the United States. Racial categories in the Dominican Republic pivot on a white/black divide, but these colors also subsume more than just skin color; this divide includes not only phenotypes, such as hair color/texture, eye color, and skin color, but also non-phenotypic factors, such as occupation, socioeconomic status, and nationality (Candelario 2007). In the Dominican Republic, social constructions of whiteness over time have come to signify modernity and progress, while those of blackness have become equated with perceptions of Haiti and Haitians (Simmons 2009; Howard 2007; García-Peña 2015).

Nationality and blackness in the Dominican Republic coalesce in the ideology of anti-Haitianism. Anti-Haitianism, or "a constellation of ideas and practices negatively affecting people (as a person or a group) from Haiti, their descendants, and those perceived as belonging to one of these groups, whether or not they actually belong" (Jayaram 2010, 33–34), is often assumed as the default position for intercultural engagement on the island of Hispaniola and has historical antecedents. The long-standing discrimination against Haitians within the Dominican Republic, deriving in part from colonial-era struggles, has affected everyday life in the Dominican Republic, both institutionally and interpersonally (Brennan 2004; Moya Pons 1998; Candelario 2007; Carruyo 2008; Gregory 2014; Schuller 2012; Keys et al. 2015). A complicated vocabulary to distinguish *dominicanidad* (Dominicanness), or what it means to be a Dominican in Spanish, has emerged not only as part of the nation-building project in the establishment of the Dominican Republic but also as a function of what García-Peña (2016, 203) asserts as the "global war on blackness." Blackness in the Dominican Republic, in effect, has become morally charged and replete with notions of particular characteristics of ethnicity, nationality, linguistics, socioeconomics, and only sometimes phenotypic traits like skin or hair color. Explanations of the ideology vary. There are those that explain anti-Haitianism as rooted in the past, as does Wucker (1999) when she refers to Dominicans and Haitians as timeless enemies; there are those who state that Dominicans "deny their black heritage" (Lamb and Dundes 2017) or have "black amnesia" (Andújar 2004); while other accounts of race and domini-canidad assert that Dominicans in fact have been denied the understanding of their African heritage because it had been criminalized and demonized by authorities within the Dominican Republic (Simmons 2009) and as a strategy of U.S. imperial intervention (García-Peña 2016). In practice, the Dominican racialized discourse effectively links the color term black (*negro*) with a nationality, being Haitian, even if their skin color may be similar to, or even lighter than, the complexions of most Dominicans (Simmons 2009, 25). This discourse produces and reproduces differences, what Wynne (2014) refers to as a mechanism of othering, created by Dominicans to distinguish themselves as socially separate from and superior to Haitians.

Across the globe, this kind of tension in multicultural contexts is not a rare phenomenon. One of the most perceptible results of the migration of people is interpersonal tension. We see this take root between nonmigrants and migrants, as well as in the ways that immigration "reform" is conceptualized and developed in policies all over the world. Tension often results between and among peoples from host and sending communities, and scholars explain the emergence of this tension using a variety of different and overlapping reasons. First, group conflict theorists explain that tension arises when people in host communities contend that migrants strain available resources, creating at least the perception of fierce competition for provisions and jobs (e.g., Blalock 1967). Second, symbolic interactionists contend that tension between people in host communities and newcomers arise when people perceive an uneven or nonexistent adoption of mainstream cultural values and practices, creating and/or reproducing misunderstandings and discrimination between host communities and migrants (e.g., Sobszak 2010). And third, other migration scholars demonstrate that tension often arises among different generations of immigrants, especially when children of migrants assimilate to some mainstream cultural values and practices, or when transnational families lament the fact that migrant family members relinquish their cultural identity and their roots, language, religion, and/or customs (e.g., Miles 2004; Sittig and González 2016). In all of these theoretical perspectives, tension is an inherent part of the migration experience for everyone as host communities and newcomers learn to live together and make sense of who they are in relation to who they are not.

Overall, these models attempting to explain the tension that results from migration assume four things: (1) that the contentious chasm between immigrants and nonimmigrants is dependent upon their differences; (2) that these differences are distinguishable and unbridgeable; (3) that the immigrants' status as different, whether the difference is rooted in social constructions of race, ethnicity, religion, or nationality, is the only characteristic of identity that comes into play in intercultural social interactions; and (4) that the presence of tension that arises with immigration signifies the absence of any other response. However, often people can hold and act upon two disparate sentiments; in other words, sometimes what people say differs from what they do. The frequently uttered phrase, "I'm not a racist, but . . ." (Blum 2002), a phrase I hear in the United States and in the Dominican Republic, reveals the difficulty of defining and problematizing the tension mounted in social environments with intercultural differences. While often people, institutions, and media highlight these difficulties, what has garnered little scholarly and popular attention are the instances of when the deeply rooted tension is suppressed or transcended. The significance of my research lies not in what Dominicans and Haitians say about each other but in how their shared responses to increasing economic hardships reveal a more nuanced and complicated narrative of if and when anti-Haitianism plays out between and among people.

Throughout my research, Dominican and Haitian participants frequently told me that they were not racists, even though I would often observe people using racist logic to characterize people of the other group (cf. Bonilla-Silva's (2014) work in the United States on "racism without racists"). In particular social venues that require intercultural interpersonal engagement, such as at church, in night school, or at places of work, Dominicans regularly distinguish themselves from Haitian migrants living and working in the Dominican Republic. However, buying food on credit in neighborhood corner stores often breaks this mold and mitigates discriminatory rhetoric and practices. In corner stores, instead of using nationality, race, or heritage (Dominican/Haitian) as a dividing line, the cultural practices of fiao require people to use class, or shared conceptions of poverty, as a significant social factor to create solidarity between people, even people belonging to different racial categories. Shopkeepers give in-store credit to people they know, but when an unknown customer asks for in-store credit, shopkeepers mitigate this risk by placing the debt of the unknown shopper on the tab of a known "responsible" person who vouches for the character of the unknown shopper. Dominican and Haitian customers at local corner stores vouch for each other to not only help people provision their households but also to create social networks that they can count on in their own times of need. I call these practices the hidden labor of fiao and explain that this labor fosters intercultural engagement.

One of the recent manifestations of anti-Haitianism has resulted in changes to long-standing immigration and citizenship policies in the Dominican Republic. Most Americans don't know much, if anything, about the history of people migrating *to* the Dominican Republic, but Americans often are aware of migration *from* the Dominican Republic. Dominican migration to the United States soared beginning in the 1980s (Portes and Rumbaut 2001), and typically, Dominicans migrated to big cities on the East Coast such as New York, Boston, or Miami. But a longer history of migration to the Dominican Republic predates this. Since 1929, the Dominican Republic has granted citizenship to all children born on Dominican soil to parents of Haitian heritage; this policy was established to attract migrant workers to work in the sugarcane fields of the Dominican Republic, much like the Bracero program in the United States between 1942 and 1964 which sought to attract migrant workers from Mexico to work in the American agricultural industry (Cohen 2013). However, in 2010, the Dominican Constitutional Ruling 0168–13 was passed, the beginning of a process that effectively annulled citizenship to residents who were born to undocumented parents who have lived and worked—often for their entire lives—in the Dominican Republic (Association of Black Anthropologists 2014; Petrozziello 2014; Rodríguez Grullón 2013). Although the ruling doesn't explicitly target Haitians, for all intents and purposes, the ruling especially affects those of Haitian heritage and more recently those who self-identify as Dominico-Haitians.

Yet in the Dominican Republic, the terms Dominico-Haitian and Haitian are complicated. These terms are not often used to self-identify but are terms either given to people by others or are declared not to exist at all. People will often refer to other people as Haitian if they have dark skin, but many Dominicans have dark skin as well. People are also referred to as Haitian when they speak Kreyol, even when they also speak Spanish, or if they speak Spanish with a heavy Kreyol accent. Moreover, many people are called Haitian even when it is known that they were born in the Dominican Republic and are referred to as Haitian just because they were born to Haitians or Haitian-descended parents. The term Dominico-Haitian, although increasingly being used to refer to people who were born in the Dominican Republic to people of Haitian heritage, is not a common term and resonates politically and socially among contemporary social movement activists who are trying to change the way citizenship and belonging is conceptualized in the Dominican Republic. In fact, during my fieldwork when I asked people how they identify themselves, just a few interviewees explicitly stated that they are "Dominico-Haitian," while many people told me that there's no such thing as "Dominico-Haitian," further evidence that Dominico-Haitian is a contested racial category.

In this book, I use interchangeably the terms race, ethnicity, heritage, and nationality when discussing characteristics of identity in Cabarete to emphasize the cultural salience of history, geography, language, citizenship, kinship, occupation, and at times some phenotypes for connoting the socially constructed differences between and among people. The concepts of race and national identity have predominated Dominican studies in a way that has eclipsed the study of life in the Dominican Republic that centers on other aspects of identity, such as gender or class (cf. Thornton and Ubiera 2019). My research shows the significance of understanding the intersections of race, ethnicity, gender, and class that have implications on the strategies people create to survive.

Martínez (2003) argues that what is commonly regarded as Dominican-Haitian tension might be something of a macro-social narrative in which government policy and/or upper-class sentiment becomes appropriated as the norm. He uses the phrase "the fatal-conflict model of Haitian-Dominican relations" to refer to tense diplomatic relations between the nations of Haiti and the Dominican Republic, but he warns that we must be careful not to generalize this tension or assume that government-level tensions play out interpersonally between and among all people. In countering academic and popular discourse of Dominican-Haitian relations (e.g., Wucker 2000), Martínez calls for a more nuanced research of Haitian-Dominican interpersonal relations and in what contexts these tensions arise:

> Much of what is not known could be discovered by going beyond survey data and analysis of elite texts to plunge into the ephemera of the everyday lives and the at times intricately encoded subjective formulations of experience of the Dominican masses . . .. In the streets, alleyways, work camps, and villages that working-class Dominicans share with Haitians are to be found little-studied perspectives on the Haitian-Dominican relationship . . . . Prolonged firsthand study in these places would reveal hitherto unsuspected complexities and might yield strongly differing interpretations . . . . We may also yet be surprised to find that most working-class Dominicans adapt more easily to the challenges of social change and show greater tolerance of racial and ethnic complexity than do their more affluent compatriots. (2003, 96)

While Dominican political policy involving immigration and citizenship may antagonize Haitian-ness in the abstract, interpersonal relations between and among Dominicans and Haitians may not be affected as such. I heeded Martínez's call by conducting my research in a relevant cultural site with intercultural (Dominican Haitian) engagement, one in which working-class and poor Dominicans and Haitians engage one another: food shopping in colmados in Cabarete, a community that is one of the primary centers of international tourism in the Dominican Republic.

Martínez's insight here may be over a decade old, but there has been little research to date that specifically questions Dominican-Haitian interpersonal relationships to examine their lived experiences. Most research in the Dominican Republic typically engages people of only one heritage or another, especially in literature on the lives of Haitians living in sugarcane plantations called *bateys* (Riveros 2014; Petrozziello 2014; Martínez 2007). Studies focusing on life in bateys further entrench the perception that migrant Haitians live in isolated, insular communities where residents have very little interaction with Dominicans. But little is known about Dominican-Haitian *intercultural*, not *intracultural*, interaction, which has become increasingly common in parts of the Dominican Republic. Kimberly Wynne's research (2014) on bateys near the northern border town of Monte Cristi is one of a handful of studies accounting for these recent changes. Wynne explains that contemporary bateys and nearby towns are intercultural places where Dominicans and Haitians live side by side. Because there is no spatial separation between groups, her work demonstrates the efforts Dominicans put into mechanisms of othering. Wynne found that working-class and poor Dominicans working and living in sugar towns and plantations "feel the pull down to the lowest rung," a rung occupied by Haitians, and "perform symbolic labor to dissociate themselves" from Haitians (Wynne 2014, 159). But she also found that Dominicans simultaneously engage in intimate and friendly relations with Haitians. Wynne's work highlights the complexity of intercultural interpersonal relationships and the need for more research in order to understand the strategies people use and under what conditions these kinds of "fictions are maintained in attempts to preserve [Dominicans'] respect" (Wynne 2014, 152). Wynne's work shows that interpersonal relations between Haitians and Dominicans are more complex than the fatal-conflict model supposes.

Maja Horn (2014) notes that ideologies such as anti-Haitianism are discursive as much as they are performative and are locked in a dialogic feedback loop, whereby reality can be shaped by discordant discourses and actions. The discordance between what people say and what people do demonstrates that contemporary anti-Haitianism in the Dominican Republic often has unexpected effects. For example, Guzmán (2016), in her research in the southern border area of Pedernales, found that

> [a]nti-Haitianism reveals itself in different ways than in places where cross-border networks are not the dominant form of relation between Dominicans and Haitians. In Pedernales, there are two Haiti's [*sic*]: the discursive Haiti that is represented as the monolithic "others" and the individual Haitians who are their friends, families, employees, customers, or neighbors. The distinction between

the two is quite significant because they demonstrate a particular reality of the border. (2016, 8)

On the island of Hispaniola, the border region is not the only geographic area where discordant discourses and actions play out. *Not Even a Grain of Rice* corroborates Wynne's and Guzmán's conclusions in a locale far from the border, in the intercultural community of Cabarete which lures migrants to work in its world-renowned tourism industry.

Living and Working in the Multicultural Community of Cabarete

The island of Hispaniola is home to two nations: the eastern two-thirds of the island is the Dominican Republic and the western one-third is Haiti. Approximately 10 million people live in each of the nations (Pan American Health Organization 2017). Cabarete is a forty-five-minute drive from the city of Puerto Plata, a city of approximately 147,000 and the capital of the state of the same name (see figure I.1). Puerto Plata is a well-known international tourist destination in its own right, known primarily for its all-inclusive resorts and as a stopping point for many Caribbean vacation cruise lines. In Cabarete, my research was conducted in two multicultural neighborhoods—Callejón

Figure I.1   Map of the Caribbean. © PeterHermesFurian/iStock/Getty Images Plus/Getty Images.

de la Loma ("Alley of the Hill" in Spanish), called the Callejón by local residents, and La Cienaga[2] ("the Swamp"). Both neighborhoods are nestled between the Caribbean Sea and a mountain chain running east-west called the Cordillera Septentrional. The Callejón is inhabited by approximately 4,000 poor and working-class Dominicans, Haitians, and a handful of international residents from primarily Europe or Canada, almost all of whom work in the area's service industry. La Cienaga is a little bit smaller in population, with about 2,500 mostly working-class and poor Dominicans and Haitians and fewer international residents than the Callejón, since La Cienaga is further away from Cabarete's city center.

Cabarete lies almost 40 kilometers east of Puerto Plata traveling east on State Highway 5, the main thoroughfare on the north coast that hugs the shoreline for most of the way (see figure I.2). To get to Cabarete from Puerto Plata, the road bisects the city of Sosúa, the site of one of the Dominican Republic's well-known red-light districts (see Brennan 2004). The most recent statistics on sex tourism in the country estimate between 25,000 and 35,000 sex workers in the Dominican Republic, the majority of whom began their work in the sex trade under the age of eighteen, often catering to international tourists (International Mission Justice 2015). In 2018, the Dominican Republic received 6.5 million tourists, and in the first months of 2019, it received almost 605,000 tourists, up by 8% from the year before. The north coastal region is one of a handful of primary tourist destinations within the country; in fact, the port of Puerto Plata, the north coast's largest city,

Figure I.2   Map of Hispaniola. Cabarete Is Located on the Point between Puerto Plata and Gaspar Hernández, on the North Shore of the Dominican Republic. © bogdanserban/iStock/Getty Images Plus/Getty Images.

is the most frequented arrival point for cruise lines entering the Dominican Republic (Dominican Ministry of Tourism 2019).

While the national language of the Dominican Republic is Spanish, on the north coast where my ethnography is set, people speak in a quick, clipped accent that is common among Caribbean Spanish speakers, with some unique regional variants that distinguish many residents as having been raised on the north coast—such as replacing the final "r" or "l" in words with a distinctive "ee" sound, turning the pronunciation of the word *amor* into "amoi," or *nacional* into "nacion-eye." The national language of Haiti is Kreyòl,[3] although most adult Haitians today were instructed in French in formal schooling. Cabarete is a town inhabited by many people from elsewhere, from other locales within the Dominican Republic, from Haiti, as well as from around the world. It is typical in downtown Cabarete to see billboard advertisements and business establishments with signs in multiple languages, including German, Russian, French, English, and Portuguese. Of the approximately 12,000 residents, about two-thirds of them have migrated to find work in Cabarete's international tourism industry (Oficina Nacional de Estadísticas 2017). As a result, everyday life for residents in the Callejón and La Cienaga is grounded in intercultural interaction.

Over 2,000 years ago, the entire island was first inhabited by primarily Arawak-speaking Taínos (Moya Pons 1998). Christopher Columbus landed on the north coast of Hispaniola on his first voyage to the Caribbean in 1492 and then in 1493 founded the north coast settlement of La Isabela. The island was colonized for almost 300 years by both the Spanish and the French, but Cabarete as a named and distinct community dates back to the early mid-1800s, during the brief period of Haitian colonization of the island (1822–1844). Schafer (2013) chronicles the founding of the region of Cabarete by the family of Zephaniah Kingsley (1765–1843), a British slave trader with a complicated socioeconomic philosophy who owned and operated plantations in southern Florida. Kingsley was enriched by his successful trading and agricultural export, the results of slave labor in Florida. He also practiced polygyny, having four common-law marriages with slaves he had subsequently freed and with whom he had nine multiracial children. He believed that agriculture could not be sustained without slave labor, but he advocated for a peculiar system of slavery in which slaves had the right to purchase their freedom over time. In the mid-1830s, when faced with strictures in Spanish Florida that outlawed "free persons of color," a distinction that included his own wives and children, Kingsley moved his family to northern Hispaniola, known at the time as Hayti, that explicably outlawed slavery as part of the new nation born of the Haitian revolutions (Torres-Saillant 2000). Here, on a bay he called Cabarete, Kingsley established an estate called Mayorasgo de Koka (Koka Estate) and bequeathed it and its operation to his son, George

Kingsley, and Zephaniah's wife and mother of George, Anna Jai Kingsley, a former slave originally from Senegal. Over time at Mayorasgo de Koka, Kingsley allowed fifty of his slaves to purchase their own freedom, running his estate on what became more of a system of indentured servitude. The estate eventually ran into disrepair, and the region of Cabarete was sparsely populated for more than a century thereafter because of its inaccessibility from the rest of the country.

Current residents in Cabarete who were born there often liked to tell me that when they were growing up, Cabarete was only a small fishing village of a couple of hundred families, connected to the rest of the country with nothing more than a dirt road. During the 1980s, a series of government administrations made tourism the cornerstone of their economic policies, and the beautiful beaches on the Dominican coast became the focal point of much private and public financial investment (Brennan 2004; Moya Pons 2011, 1998; Gregory 2014), including the construction of the northern highway from Puerto Plata to the Samaná peninsula. Cabarete has not been invaded by large multinational resorts which are found in nearby Puerto Plata, or like those much further away in the community of Punta Cana on the southeastern coast. But during my research, Cabarete did consist of beachfront hotels that, like other areas of the Dominican Republic, attract both international and domestic tourists. Over time, the neighborhoods of the Callejón and La Cienaga grew to house residents who work in low-wage positions in restaurants, gift shops, and hotels, as clerks, food servers, gardeners, cleaning staff, translators, and guides.

Composing a life in the Callejón and La Cienaga is a process of piecing together as many various income generating opportunities as possible at different times of the year, as the tourist seasons ebb and flow according to the holiday calendars in the Global North and in the Dominican Republic. While there are a handful of residents who form part of the area's small middle class, primarily working in schools, NGOs, or managing small tourist shops, the majority living and working in these neighborhoods are part of the underemployed service industry sector who either work behind the scenes or directly with tourists to maintain Cabarete's reputation for being what some people have called "the Disneyland of the Dominican Republic," because of its reputation as a vacation destination. Low wages and difficult working conditions do not deter people from migrating to Cabarete, which is evidenced by the throngs of people moving to and from the area to look for work. This makes for a very busy place, even during the slowest economic times of the year. The Callejón and La Cienaga do not have ethnic enclaves, no areas known as Little Haiti like those found in the capital of Santo Domingo (Mateo 2017). Instead, life in Cabarete is fundamentally integrated, a place where people from all over the world work and live side by side, having implications for how they build social networks and develop strategies, such as buying food on credit in local corner stores, to help them cope with the uncertainties of living in a precarious place.

FIAO, GENTE RESPONSABLE, AND COLMADOS

Since the early 2000s, food prices in the Dominican Republic have steadily outpaced what people earn (Food and Agriculture Organization 2016), which has caused the most strain among the working poor. For those struggling to maintain household food security, or the "availability and adequate access at all times to sufficient, safe, nutritious food to maintain a healthy and active life" (World Food Programme 2017), gaining access to in-store credit has become an increasingly pervasive and commonplace economic strategy to secure household food needs. Fiao links Dominicans and Haitians in extensive social networks that are built upon borrowers' reputations of being *gente responsable* (responsible people, those who are good to their word and pay off their debt). By bringing together those who are deemed "responsible," fiao provides a cultural site in which Haitians and Dominicans establish networks so that they can garner household food needs.

Fiao is used in small, neighborhood corner stores called *colmados* in Dominican Spanish. Although large grocery stores exist in the Dominican Republic, colmados are the primary shopping venues for all residents in the Dominican Republic, especially for the working poor. As a frame of reference, these neighborhood corner stores are like those in the United States that are often referred to as mini-markets or *bodegas*, a word common in the Spanish-speaking Caribbean, such as Puerto Rico and Cuba. They are small (usually no more than 15 × 30 meters) grocers and are ubiquitous throughout both rural and urban areas of the Dominican Republic. Typically, they carry a variety of bulk vegetables and fruits for sale, stored in wooden shelves or plastic flats, and are often sold by unit instead of by weight, such as beets, carrots, tomatoes, onions, garlic, cabbage, potatoes, cucumbers, limes, lemons, as well as Caribbean vegetables such as, *auyama* (pumpkin), *tayota*, and yucca. Colmados also sell bulk products, such as different grains of rice, laundry detergent, and beans (known as *habichuelas* throughout the Caribbean). These products are sold by weight, but the customary practice is for shoppers to buy a set amount of each bulk product, usually 15, 20, 25, or 50 pesos per unit (during my fieldwork, the peso conversion rate was approximately RD44/US$1). Colmados sell homemade foods prepared by the shopkeeper or other residents, typically sold during morning hours. These cooked foods are usually baked buns or small loaves of bread, homemade pastries such as cornmeal flour and cheese-filled *arepas* or small meat hand-pies called

Figure I.3   A Typical Colmado. Photo taken by the author.

empanadas, small candies that resemble caramels, and stewed beans sold in small bags. Colmados also offer industrially processed foods, such as canned vegetables, evaporated milk (a staple for many dishes), cassava bread (yucca flatbread), tinned meats, and canned beans. Also, different varieties of local rum, sweet wines, and sundries such as toilet paper, laundry detergent, feminine hygiene products, dominoes (a common pastime), and vacuum-packed cartons of milk and juices are sold. Colmados also carry individually wrapped products, such as disposable razors, small packets of vanilla extract and other spices (such as cinnamon, anise, cloves, and curry), cocoa powder, and the omnipresent culinary ingredient: chicken bouillon in cubes or in liquid form to season any Dominican or Haitian dish. Customers can also purchase bagged ice and cold drinks from large coolers, such as local and international soft drinks, liter bottles of local beer served with plastic cups to share with others, and 5-gallon jugs of potable drinking water, like the one I observed in Teresa's home.

Most colmados sell eggs, and some also sell meat, primarily chicken, usually butchered right on the spot for custom orders.

Sometimes, shopkeepers maintain a chicken coop in the backyard of the colmado, a less expensive way for the shopkeeper to keep eggs and meat on hand for sale. Colmados typically have a large freezer and/or refrigerator

Figure I.4   Shopkeeper Butchering a Chicken for a Custom Order. Photo taken by the author.

behind the front counter in which to store dairy products and meats, as well as small popsicles and ice creams on a stick which are sold for just a few pesos.

Like some bodegas in urban areas in the United States, colmados often make deliveries on motor scooters to people who have phoned in their orders. Some colmados, labeled *colmadones*, become dancehalls at night. Shopkeepers open their doors well into the evening hours, turn up *merengue* or *bachata* (typical Dominican music), and provide beer and rum to patrons who come to chat, dance, eat, and engage in common Dominican pastimes such as playing dominoes or pool. As both corner stores and dancehalls, colmados are significant cultural sites for people to socially and economically gather.

Shopping in colmados using fiao in the Dominican Republic does not mean food is purchased using a debit or credit card. Colmados do not have credit card machines. Credit cards are scarce and nonexistent among working-class customers who frequently shop almost exclusively in neighborhood colmados. Fiao is also not a micro-loan. Fiao is unlike micro-loans in two very important respects: (1) fiao is not the act of lending money so that people can start business enterprises; fiao is a loan to buy food and other sundries. And (2) there is no interest added to purchases made with fiao; these debts are for exactly what was purchased. Instead, fiao functions when colmado owners, known as *colmaderos* or *colmaderas* in Spanish (depending on the gender of the shopkeeper), decide whether to allow customers to buy their food on credit. Purchases are recorded by hand in a notebook, and customers who owe money to shopkeepers must pay at least part of their debt in a timely manner. If they fail to do so, their requests to continue to buy their food on a tab will be denied.

Shopkeepers, too, maintain their supplies using fiao with food distributors, so if customers fail to repay their debt to shopkeepers, then colmaderos are unable to pay their own debts to distributors. The cycle of indebtedness among customers, shopkeepers, and distributors is fragile, and this fragility, in part, sometimes can lead to colmados' financial ruin. Colmados with long lines outside of their shops in the late morning hours, such as those that I would often see outside of Pepe's colmado, one of the colmados referred to in Teresa's conversation with me, were those that were financially healthy because their supply could keep up with customers' demand. However, several colmados regularly display bare shelves and empty food bins, and the primary reason for this scarcity is that shopkeepers are not repaid so that they could, in turn, repay their own debts and stock their shelves. Therefore, shopkeepers have an extremely important task that has far-reaching consequences: attracting customers to shop at their stores, enticing them with the promise of buying food on credit, but knowing which customers will or will not be able to pay their debts in a timely manner so that their shops can remain financially solvent. Shopkeepers' role in determining who is allowed to buy food on credit is much like the process of determining a credit score in the United States. Credit scores are analytic measures of risk determined by potential borrowers' ability to pay off their debts on a reliable timeline. Shopkeepers in the Dominican Republic use the credibility of others to help them determine who is and who is not worth the risk. My book shows that in colmados, determining who is credit-worthy is a social process that brings people together into webs of relationships that people draw upon in times of need.

Recent scholarship on food security in the Dominican Republic has focused on strategies Dominicans use to purchase food (e.g., Murray 1996; Rosing 2007, 2009). But there has been little research to date discussing household food security among Haitians living and working in the Dominican Republic. The gap in this literature is noteworthy because of the broader contemporary social context of tension between resident Dominicans and people of Haitian descent in the Dominican Republic. Overlooking the role of colmados and shopping habits in the cultural context of the Dominican Republic is a surprising gap in our understanding not only because corner stores are essential to mitigating the hardship of rising food prices on poor people in the Dominican Republic but also because corner stores thrive in the imaginary of popular culture. For example, in the Dominican film *Sanky Panky* (2007), the protagonist is an upwardly mobile shopkeeper and the first scene in the film depicts typical customer-shopkeeper transactions in the colmado in which he works. Colmados are also featured in popular music, such as the song, "Colmado," from Janio Lora's 2015 album *Mi Nueva Edad*, the lyrics of which highlight the vitality of everyday activities, both social and economic, revolving in and around colmados, such as meeting with friends:

> Hello, corner store/Bring me four cold beers/Dominoes will be played/A frosty beer bottle, dressed as a bride/How it smokes, it sings, to please . . ..

Or for entertainment and to leave work behind:

> Hey there, baby, turn around for me/Turn for me, shake your booty/To the corner store where the air's fresher/What dancing, how lovely, what love! (Lora, featuring Xiomara Fortuna 2015)

Corner stores have an important role to play in the social reproduction of place, the processes and mechanisms by which a society transforms and maintains its social order and relations across time and space. Corner stores in the Dominican Republic provide a culturally salient intersection between food, space, and place which I use as a lens to examine intercultural relationships. The links between borrowers and creditors—customers, storekeepers, and distributors—in colmados are at the center of social and economic life in the Dominican Republic. In the Dominican Republic, the varieties and rules of fiao exchanges create a local moral economy or cultural norms within a system of economic exchange. The rules governing social norms in contemporary food shopping practices, especially the local practice of buying food on credit in corner stores, run counter to the assumed norms of typical Haitian Dominican interactions in other cultural venues in the Dominican Republic. The development of contemporary racial discourse in the Dominican Republic revolves around shifting perceptions of race, citizenship, and belonging and has implications for our understanding of everyday experiences of racism, especially in intercultural places and spaces.

FOOD SHOPPING, DEBT, AND THE
BOUNDARIES OF MORAL PERSONHOOD

Buying food on credit is not unique to the Dominican Republic; neither is incurring debt to feed the family. In-store credit has been used throughout history in different global contexts and has been documented in oral histories, such as the cultural practice of "trust" in Syrian and Chinese neighborhoods in Trinidad (Charlene Roach, personal communication), as well as U.S.-based written historical accounts (Poe 1999) and in fiction (Smith 2001 [1943], 106, 122). Literature on colonial practices around the world reveals that one of the most predictable facets of colonialism was perpetual indebtedness of colonized populations, those who worked on plantations and in mines as virtual or actual slaves, in company stores owned and operated by colonizers (Moore Lappé and Collins 1977; Klein 2011; Thorp 2012). Debt peonage became a signature component of colonialism around the globe, predicated upon using food shopping and specific food shops as important factors in the maintenance of the colonial exploitation of poor workers. Colonizers replaced local diversified agricultural practices, substituting them with the production of cash crops such as coffee, sugar, rice, and tea. Food was then imported from the metropole to company stores in the periphery, in which people used in-store credit to provision households, spawning a cycle of indebtedness that at once tethered people to the company store and increased the metropole's sale of goods.

Research on purchasing food with in-store credit also reveals the political implications of shopping habits within specific types of venues (Deutsch 2001). Buying food on credit may seem like an extremely beneficial strategy for customers, but there are some clear challenges posed by this socioeconomic system of exchanges, particularly in small communities or close-knit neighborhoods where social ties are cemented and maintained via these networks of exchanges. For example, in her study of African American shopping habits in Chicago from 1915 to 1947, Poe (1999) found that African American customers frequented white local grocers not only because of the perception that these shops often had higher quality items than African American shops, but white grocers "would punish" African American shoppers who failed to exhibit store loyalty by cutting off their in-store credit lines.

Attending to food shopping as a politicized process means not only paying attention to bidirectional, macro-economic relations (e.g., colonized vs. colonizers) as well as interpersonal relations (e.g., white shopkeepers vs. black customers), but it can also unveil moral economies grounded in a variety of agendas and relationships between and among multiple actors. For example, in contemporary urban Detroit, Jung and Newman (2014) suggest that competing claims to control the moral economy are often articulated by diverse actors. In Detroit, various community stakeholders proposed diverse perspectives on ethical food and ethical food practices which were negotiated and mediated through a number of factors: neoliberal consumer politics (a focus on the individual), norms of local governance (care for one's neighborhood), and "Detroit's historically racialized, crisis-ridden body politic" (Jung and Newman 2014). These negotiations gave rise to varying conceptualizations of morality, including how to evaluate the quality of items, what it means to care for the community, and how to assess a fair price of goods.

Colloquially, morality is defined as a system of determining right and wrong, good and bad. And since the beginning of anthropology as a discipline, anthropologists have provided ethnographic analysis of morality as unique collective cultural constructions of what constitutes good, bad, obligation, duty, or responsibility, or what is right or just, in everyday experiences. For example, Miller (2001) examined shopping as a moral experience and found contradictions among British shoppers in North London as they discussed their justifications and desires. His interviewees often spoke of their desire to engage in what Miller regarded as ethical shopping or decision-making built upon forsaking the immediate concerns of the household in return for the greater collective social good (such as fairness for food service workers or good working conditions for agricultural laborers). But these shoppers were more apt in practice to engage in moral shopping, in which shopping decisions were made in order to maximize economic savings for their families. Miller concluded that people are not "hypocritical or deluded" (Miller 2001) but instead are operating in different "semi-autonomous fields" with regard to their social connections to kin, community, and other aspects of identity. Overall, Miller found that relationships to kin, community, and identity, respectively, govern shopping habits, which may seem contradictory but, in essence, relate to these different spheres of people's lives. And sometimes, discrepancies emerge between what people say and what people actually do as they formulate positions, desires, and justifications around the boundaries of moral experiences.

Recently, morality has garnered additional attention in anthropology, challenging research to move beyond a cultural particularist perspective to focus instead on how individuals live within the moral experience and how these moral judgments and experiences change over time. Zigon and Throop's (2014, 2–3) volume posits an anthropology of morality as an approach to ethnography that "come[s] to understand how one lives through and by moral experience":

[A] person-centered perspective on experience highlights processes of subject formation and the moral shaping of our experience of the world. Experience, in this sense of the term, leads us to examine how moral dispositions and ethical assumptions impact what we notice, how we react, who we love and hate, the attachments we acquire, the motives and desires that move us to act, the situations, relationships, activities, and orientations that we habitually take up . . . . Our experiences of the world and how we might struggle to transform those experiences, to rethink them, to reinterpret them, to reinhabit them, and to reposition ourselves variously as sufferers or actors on the differing scenes that in part constitute our social existence, is also an aspect of moral experience. (Zigon and Throop 2014, 8)

Individuals with the same positionalities living within the same moral experience, "the same object, situation, state of affairs, action, or quality . . . , depending on the context at hand," may perceive and experience it in myriad ways at different times, what Zigon and Throop (2014, 13) call "plural singularities" (13). Morality is not only personally experienced but is also embroiled within broader structures of power (Van Vleet 2019). Zigon and Throop (2014) remind us that morality is a processual experience, affected by individuals' positions in historical, social, economic, political, and cultural contexts. *Not Even a Grain of Rice* builds on this research, showing that local demographic shifts have created new moral discourses of debt, built upon understandings of care for the self and care for others.

RESEARCH DESIGN AND STRUCTURE OF THE BOOK

One of the strengths of anthropological research lies in its ability to shed light on the importance of everyday practices that often are overlooked by others (Corr 2016). With this in mind, *Not Even a Grain of Rice* has been written for a wide audience. The book has been written for anthropologists and other scholars of food studies, culture change, race and citizenship, and Latin America and the Caribbean to fill gaps in our understanding of food provisioning in areas that are experiencing cultural change due to recent immigration. But the book has also been written with an eye toward undergraduate students or readers who are less familiar with the region and the dynamics of economies shaped by colonial legacies. My hope is that these readers gain an appreciation for the complexity of intercultural interactions and people's ingenuity and tenacity in the face of life's challenges.

The title of this book is taken from a commonly uttered phrase in the Dominican Republic. As Garth (2020) describes about food in Cuba, rice is an essential component in any Dominican meal; without rice on the plate, most people would not view it as a real meal. In Cabarete, the phrase, "ni un grano de arroz," (not even a grain of rice) is not only used when people haven't eaten yet that day (as in, "I've eaten not even a grain of rice today"), but it is also used as a lament about the lapse of people's socioeconomic obligations to each other (as in, "I've not even eaten a grain of rice today because no one vouched for me so that I could buy food on credit"). As I have done so in this introduction, each chapter of the book begins with an excerpt from my ethnographic fieldnotes, a story that provides a window into and analysis of pertinent themes and issues. The title of each chapter incorporates relevant quotes from research participants which characterize the objective of the chapter.

The fieldwork that I conducted to write *Not Even a Grain of Rice* was carried out in the summers of 2011 and 2013 and during a year-long sabbatical I was awarded during the 2014–2015 academic year. Participant observation, focus groups, and in-depth interviews were my primary research methods. Participant observation was crucial to my research because it helped foster rapport between me, an outsider, and shoppers and shopkeepers. Developing long-term relationships with local residents allowed me to minimize problems with validity in ethnographic research. Interviewees often underreported intercultural tension or discrimination in Cabarete; when this occurred, I would challenge the interviewee with anecdotal evidence of what I had seen and heard during my fieldwork. These challenges were usually met with a more complicated rendering of intercultural relations in Cabarete, one that included their own experiences of racism and intercultural solidarity. Another tactic that proved essential to gaining rapport with people was discussing my own country's problems with racism and immigration; as noted in the preface to this book, highlighting racial tension and struggles in the United States showed residents that I did not purport to have any sort of moral high ground or indicate that I was trying to be didactic in my research. In fact, interviewees frequently told me that discussing racism in the United States showed them that I recognized our shared problems.

Out of a total of twenty-six colmados in both neighborhoods, twelve shopkeepers allowed me to conduct weekly fieldwork in their corner stores, in which I observed shopping patterns, such as goods people purchased and customer-shopkeeper interactions, and interviewed shopkeepers and customers. Additionally, nine of the shopkeepers who allowed me to conduct participant observation in their colmados permitted me access to read and review their fiao *cuadernos*, the notebooks in which customers' tabs are documented. Overall, I interviewed fourteen different colmaderos and eighty-one customers, all of whom discussed fiao lending and borrowing practices in great detail. My interviews with colmaderos revolved around the origin of their colmados, the process of becoming a shopkeeper, their relationships with employees and distributors, and everyday purchasing and lending practices. With customers, my interviewees discussed their decision-making processes about where they shopped, why, and how often they frequented particular colmados, and how they engaged in fiao.

Because participant observation in anthropological fieldwork requires researchers to learn the languages of the people they study, my research was conducted in the language of choice of my participants: I am a fluent Spanish speaker, and I learned enough Haitian Kreyòl in order to conduct interviews and learn more about the lives of Haitian participants, especially those who had just recently migrated to the area. All names in the book are pseudonyms to protect individuals' identities, and at times I have modified some details of events and places to help preserve people's privacy.

To contextualize the information I gleaned in colmados, I conducted participant observation, focus groups, and interviews in other social venues within Cabarete, sites that gave me insight into other spheres of life: a Haitian Christian church; the area's adult night school; a local language school; and three nongovernmental organizations (NGO) located in Cabarete. I interviewed church members and administrators, adult night school teachers and students, language school teachers and students, a local school director, and NGO personnel and participants. And I conducted two focus groups with students and teachers at a local language school, where Dominican adults took classes in German and English to give them marketable skills in the local tourism economy. These methods allowed me to compare and contrast intercultural interaction that I encountered in everyday life in Cabarete.

Carrying out research on debt and provisioning households came with some inherent difficulties. First, Cabarete, like a lot of the Dominican Republic, is a community where very few of the working poor are issued checks as payment for their work, make direct deposits of their pay, or even have bank accounts. Beyond people's self-reporting, I had to find creative ways to verify people's salaries and household incomes. To cross-check household incomes, I interviewed both workers and employers when possible. Yet sometimes there were discrepancies between what workers and employers reported. When this occurred, I took the averages of the two and reported these figures in the book.

Second, as other ethnographers have reported in their own research in colmados, such as Murray's in-depth ethnographic work in two colmados in Santo Domingo (1996), it was difficult to get permission from area shopkeepers to review their books so I had a sense of colmados' volume of inventory or their profit margins. While shopkeepers were reluctant to allow me access to their accounting, they did permit me access to engage in so much of the lives of their colmados, including reviewing their notebooks which documented in-store credit. Some of the colmados that were included in this study are unregistered, and therefore not legally operating, so shopkeepers were naturally wary to offer up a review of their books. But shopkeepers had no problem allowing me to review their fiao notebooks, in no small part because it demonstrated their community-minded generosity, as they either inferred or told me outright. Therefore, *Not Even a Grain of Rice* does not provide an in-depth economic rendering of the role of colmados in this community but instead highlights fiao as a set of socioeconomic practices and the social implications fiao has in a multicultural community like Cabarete.

Third, a limitation of my study is that it may not be generalizable within the Dominican Republic. At the time of this writing, Cabarete is a unique Dominican community, one of just a handful of multicultural small cities or urban neighborhoods—which was exactly why I wanted to conduct the study there in the first place. Even though Cabarete is located not too far from the border, it is a long journey by bus—usually including multiple bus transfers. Therefore, when people migrate to Cabarete, they tend to stay. And since the only segregation that exists in Cabarete revolves not around the Haitian Dominican divide but around the divide between international tourists and low-income workers, people who migrate to Cabarete tend to live in the multicultural neighborhoods that they can afford, which are the Callejón and La Cienaga. Outside of life in bateys, most of what we know about Haitians' experiences in the Dominican Republic stem from studies conducted in communities along the border, or in Santo Domingo, such as in the neighborhood known as Little Haiti. This research shows that in these locales, Haitians not only experience discrimination, but they also fail to create community since their stays in these locales are ephemeral. For example, in her long-term ethnographic study of Little Haiti in Santo Domingo, Mateo (2017) concludes that Little Haiti in Santo Domingo is little more than a transit stop for Haitians who move on to other cities to pursue jobs throughout the Dominican Republic. And along the border, especially at the beginning of my fieldwork in 2011, Haitians would regularly participate in daily life in the Dominican Republic—usually by selling or shopping at Dominican markets—but then return home to Haiti in the evening. Therefore, in both locales—in border communities and in Little Haiti—Haitians and Dominicans have typically had limited experience with reaching across difference and creating lasting intercultural relations. Research in locales where intercultural relations are brokered, such as Wynne's (2014) work on intercultural bateys near Monte Cristi and Guzmán's (2016) research in Dajabón, is beginning to chip away at the gap of what we know about interpersonal relations between Dominicans and Haitians. My hope is that, like this recent research in other areas of the Dominican Republic, *Not Even a Grain of Rice* helps to fill this gap.

The greatest challenge that I faced in the Dominican Republic was entirely a product of my own making because of the focus of my research. To update our understanding of what it means to live, work, and belong in the Dominican Republic, this book uses stories people shared with me about their journey to Cabarete and the accommodations they have had to make along the way to live and work there—not only material accommodations, such as under what conditions they live and work, but also accommodations about their identities and fundamental aspects of how they create connections with others in a locale, where they are surrounded by so much difference. To this end, sometimes the stories in this book might use words, phrases, or depictions of others that are shocking to readers. They were, in fact, shocking to me. I grew up in a large, multiracial family in an ethnically and racially diverse city in Massachusetts, where I was born and raised for the first twenty-two years of my life. My siblings and I experienced interpersonal racism from others, and we were keenly aware that not everyone understood our family. Being a part of a multiracial family created by biology and adoption in the 1980s was complicated and misunderstood; we didn't often make sense to people whose understanding of a family was a web of social relations tied together through "blood or marriage" (Schneider 1980). When I showed photos of my family of origin to Dominicans and Haitians during my fieldwork, they would observe the different skin hues, hair textures, and eye colors of my family and often ask me some version of the proverbial question, "What are you?"—referring to our ethnic heritage—especially because many Dominicans and Haitians have family members with a wide variety of these phenotypes. But it was when I interviewed research participants or conducted participant observation in their everyday lives that challenged me the most. When Dominican research participants talked about Haitians, and Haitians talked about Dominicans, they frequently would use derogatory, racist generalizations to characterize the other group, such as "all Haitians are thieves" or "all Dominicans are lazy dogs." Throughout the course of my fieldwork, people would make statements like these and sometimes act in kind, but often these same people would create genuine and meaningful relationships with Others; this is the disconnect upon which this book is based.

However, this book is not an apology for racism. In *Not Even a Grain of Rice*, chapters tackle separate but intertwined issues that relate to learning more about the ways that racism is invoked and/or acted upon, an important contribution to understanding contemporary Dominican Haitian interpersonal relations, especially in light of social movement activism, both in Hispaniola and abroad, that is trying to expose policies and practices that discriminate against persons of Haitian descent living and working in the Dominican Republic. Chapter 1, "'I'm Not a Racist, But. . .': Friction, Anti-Haitianism, and Everyday Intercultural Relations in Cabarete," chronicles the history of anti-Haitianism on the island of Hispaniola that is based upon the clear divide between Dominican and Haitian and details the contemporary social consequences of this divide. Using the data gleaned from the adult night school, the Haitian church, the local language school, and NGOs, chapter 1 also discusses the range of responses that Dominicans and Haitians express about residents' usage of mechanisms of othering. Chapter 2, "'Everything Is Cheaper at the Supermarket, But I Can't Afford It': Colmados as a Total Social Phenomenon," provides a history of the ubiquity of colmados in the Dominican Republic and the rise of the dichotomy between supermarkets as *lo extranjero* (the foreign) and colmados as *lo criollo* (the homegrown).

Chapter 2 also offers in-depth ethnography of typical shopping experiences in colmados, including an analysis of the dynamics based upon gender and kinship as shoppers, shopkeepers, and delivery staff engage in the everyday labor of making a living and provisioning their households. Chapter 3, "'Pa' la Dignidad': Fiao and the Emergent Moralities of Being Responsible," describes the three different types of fiao practices in Cabarete and the hidden labor involved with creating networks of borrowers and creditors that people can count on in times of need. Chapter 3 links fiao to conceptions of responsibility and hard work and argues that new emergent moralities are being defined in Cabarete based upon these conceptions. Chapter 4, "'The Door Is Always Open . . . Until It Isn't': The Hidden Labor of Becoming Gente Responsable," describes the process of becoming gente responsable and how, at times, those who were once considered responsible fail to secure in-store credit. This chapter also discusses the failure of colmados themselves, when shopkeepers overlend and are unable to repay their own loans to distributors, resulting in a cycle of shopkeepers being denied fiao, decreased inventory to sell, and fewer customers to buy. Colmaderos, therefore, become the cornerstone of the very fragile system of lending and borrowing in Cabarete. In the conclusion, "'Fíame Por Favor': Ties That Bind in Cabarete," I summarize the book's main arguments and the significance of the results in Cabarete has for our understanding of how intercultural, migrant-hosting communities negotiate and contest inequality more generally.

The analysis of fiao in this book provides the necessary framework to piece together why Teresa, in the opening story of this chapter, reacted the way that she did and what all of the pieces of this puzzle mean. Teresa was first granted fiao from three area colmados, two of which were Pepe's and Ana's, because she was the wife of Wilman, a highly respected individual because he had not one but two jobs in the local tourism industry. He had earned the reputation as gente responsable because his two jobs allowed him to pay off his debt. When Wilman had trouble paying his debt, he often asked his friend Ricardo for a small loan. Wilman rarely had to resort to this, but when the local tourism season was slow, Wilman was not paid on time, or at all, and couldn't pay his debts in corner stores. When I wrote this chapter's initial fieldnotes story, Teresa and Wilman had extra debts to pay because of her recent surgery and recovery-related events. Therefore, Wilman and Teresa were finding it difficult to pay off their debts, and colmaderos took notice. On top of all of this, the perfect storm had just come in: at the time, Ricardo, a Dominican who had migrated to Cabarete from the capital and had been living in El Callejón for four years, hadn't worked on a construction crew for over two months, so Teresa and Wilman couldn't count on him for a loan to help them pay their bills. Within a month and a half, Teresa and Wilman had missed three payments on their debts to all three colmados. Therefore, Teresa was concerned that if she and I shopped for bouillon that day, one of two things would have occurred: (1) if she had asked to put the purchase on her tab, the colmaderos may have denied her on the basis that she had exhausted their good will or (2) if she had allowed me to pay for the bouillon, the colmaderos may have expected me to pay off the entire debt that she owed for the last month and a half. Both of these scenarios made her uncomfortable.

In the end, Teresa risked it, decided to shop at Ana's colmado, and asked me to pay for the bouillon. Ana is a thirty-six-year-old Haitian colmadera, whose colmado was spiraling into financial ruin, due in part to people who couldn't pay their bills, like Teresa and Wilman. When we arrived at Ana's colmado, she accepted the cash I gave her for the bouillon and did not require that I pay off Teresa's debt. As we walked back to Teresa's house to complete our meal preparation, I asked her to guess why Ana didn't ask me to pay for her full tab. Teresa responded, "that's because she's a woman," as if that was supposed to clear everything up for me. *Not Even a Grain of Rice* shows that patriarchy plays a role in how fiao relationships are solidified, but fiao also simultaneously fosters solidarity among women, a feminist ethics of care (Gilligan and Noddings 2009). I use intersectionality (Crenshaw 1989) to conceptualize the relations between multiple systems of oppression, including race, gender, social class, and nationalism, that construct identities and positionalities related to power and privilege.

Stories like Teresa's in this book demonstrate that buying food on credit in corner stores is a complex process, signaling a new shift about how working-class people perceive, understand, work against, and work within difference. The process of creating socioeconomic relationships across boundaries gives me some hope in a world that is presently reconciling historical and contemporary racism. But this book shows us that fiao is not enough; while helpful in the short term to buy food, using in-store credit does not lift people out of poverty, neither customers nor shopkeepers. In this international tourism destination, fiao simultaneously works to mitigate the effects of racist rhetoric but maintains a system of economic oppression and exploitation: people who have a difficult time putting food on the table for their families are those very same people who provide the necessary structure of less expensive services to people who are financially better-off, both visitors from within the Dominican Republic and from abroad.

NOTES

1. In Spanish, *don* (for men) and *doña* (for women) are terms of address, much like Mr. and Mrs./Ms., except a little less formal. These terms of address are followed by the person's first name, not their last name, as in the case of doña Marisa here.

2. Typically, the Spanish word *ciénaga* has an accent over the "e." Yet, the name of this neighborhood is spelled without the accent, so I use this spelling throughout the book.

3. Kreyòl is the Haitian spelling of its language. The Anglicized spelling of this word is "Creole."

Chapter 1

"I'm Not a Racist, But . . ."

Friction, Anti-Haitianism, and Everyday Intercultural Relations in Cabarete

24 June 2013

"Vamos," cried the doorman, as he banged twice on the roof of the white Toyota van, climbing back onto the bus and then hanging on, half in/half out of the bus as it was moving. Teresa and I were traveling on a local bus, called a guagua *in the Dominican Republic, to Sosúa, about a 30-minute ride from the Callejón, stopping every few minutes to pick someone up from the side of the road. Our plan was to shop at the* pulga, *the Dominican word for an open-air market where a wide variety of things are sold, from butchered meats and produce to second-hand clothes, curios, and athletic equipment. In English, pulga literally means flea; when someone says that they're going to the pulga, it metaphorically refers to the flea market. On the bus that day, there were 20 people, not including two infants—one laying and the other sitting on their mothers' laps—piled into the guagua that should have seated a maximum of only 12 people comfortably in its four rows of bench seating. Dominican bus drivers hire young men, usually between the ages of 16–30, as doormen who stand by the open sliding side door on the running buses not only to recruit passengers but also to manage seating arrangements in the van. Being a passenger on an overcrowded bus means that passengers are continuously moving around, changing seats as they disembark and then re-embark the bus to let other passengers off at their stops. This means that unless they end up sitting on the side of the bus furthest from the door, sometimes passengers lose their seat or have to change seats as they ride to their destination. This is a normal and expected, albeit unpleasant, fact of life using public transportation.*

Two of the passengers that day were two women in their early 20s who were speaking Kreyòl to each other. They had been on the bus already when Teresa and I flagged it down at the entrance of the Callejón, and they were

31

seated behind the driver in the often coveted seat by the window (coveted, unless the doorman tries to put five people in the bench seat made for three, and then passengers end up squashed against the window). An elderly woman and her adult son flagged down our bus by the side of the road with a swipe of the man's raised hand, and the doorman whistled and banged the roof of the van one time to alert the driver to pick them up. As we were approaching the new passengers, the doorman told everyone in the bench seat behind the driver, "Everyone out!" This sometimes happens so that passengers who have physical challenges—issues that would encumber them getting on and off the bus multiple times to let others out at their stops—are seated behind the driver as to not hamper the doorman's job of keeping the bus running smoothly and efficiently. But when the side door opened and the other two passengers seated in that row got out as the doorman requested, the two Kreyòl-speakers looked at each other and remained seated. Standing at the door, the doorman scowled at the two seated women and repeated, "Listen, everyone out!" This time, one of the Kreyòl-speakers shook her head and softly said, "No." There were "tsks" coming from some of the other passengers, loudly enough so that the whole bus could hear them. The adult son who was waiting to get on the bus looked at the Kreyòl-speakers and said in Spanish, "Negritas, my mother is old and feeble, and she needs to sit there all the way to Puerto Plata [the city about 30 minutes east of Sosúa]." The Kreyòl-speaker closest to the window rolled her eyes and replied in Kreyòl-inflected Spanish, "Last time I was on this bus, the bus was too crowded and someone hanging out the door fell into me when the bus stopped fast. That hurt," and neither woman moved to get off the bus. The doorman then said, "Negras, if you don't get out to let this elderly woman on, you won't get back on this bus," to which the women both got off reluctantly to let the new passengers take their seats.

Teresa and I looked at each other knowingly as passengers reshuffled into a new seating arrangement. From where we were sitting, we could hear grumbles from passengers because of the short delay that the refusal had effected. The Kreyòl-speakers were now seated close to the door, sitting precariously close to the doorman who was hanging out of the door calling out the bus route to attract potential passengers. As the bus pulled away, one of the Kreyòl-speakers started complaining loudly, without looking at anyone in particular: "Don't you fall into me as we ride!" The doorman poked his head in the bus and, looking straight at the complaining woman, responded with, "Cool it, I'm a professional [Tranquílate, yo soy professional]! You Haitians are all the same: you come here and take up space. You don't deserve to be here! You don't belong here! Your next bus should be the one to Dajabón [the northern entry point on the Dominican-Haitian border]!" No one said a word. Teresa looked at me and shook her head almost imperceptibly and scrunched up her mouth as she nodded toward the doorman. Her look told me that she had heard this before and didn't like it.

"La 'quina" [a common abbreviation of "la esquina," or at the corner], I announced to the doorman when we approached our stop. After the requisite reshuffling of passengers seated in front of us near the door, we got out of the guagua and started walking toward the entrance of the pulga. "What did you think of that?" I asked Teresa as we neared the first stall in the market. "Yes, well, that happens all the time. They [the Kreyòl-speakers] should have gotten out to help that old woman, but it's typical that they got scolded and were told to go back to Haiti. I know those women. They sometimes come to our church. And they are not from Haiti, or they haven't been for a long time . . . . I don't know, but I think they have lived here all their lives. They just speak Kreyòl when they don't want other people to understand them!"

About a half-hour later, we bumped into a couple in the pulga who we knew from La Cienaga, Angelica and David, two Dominicans who had moved to La Cienaga three years ago from Los Aguayos, a working-class neighborhood outside of Santiago. David works as a gardener in a house next door to the house Teresa's husband, Wilman, works in as a gardener. I re-told the story of what happened to the two women on the bus, and David and Angelica were not at all sympathetic to the women's plight. "She should have gotten off the bus to let the poor old woman on," cried David. "Why do you all do that?" he said, looking at Teresa and expecting her to speak on behalf of the two women because Teresa is Haitian. Teresa didn't respond, but Angelica's eyes got wide and she looked at me and said, "I'm not a racist, but Haitians are very impolite [maleducados]. *That's just not polite [not giving the old woman their seat]." Teresa maintained her silence.*

The above story is but one example of many during my fieldwork that called attention to interpersonal tension between Haitians and Dominicans in Cabarete. During my twelve months of working there, I witnessed thirty-four different encounters between Dominicans and the people of Haitian descent that revolved around race, racism, and belonging; additionally, I heard some version of the phrase uttered by Angelica, "I'm not a racist, but . . . ," a total of fifteen times by residents in the Callejón and La Cienaga. The incident between the doorman and the two bus passengers was not a unique occurrence; the story of interpersonal tension involving Teresa, Angelica, and David was also not exceptional, inasmuch as Angelica and David directly questioned Teresa to speak on behalf of all Haitians about someone else's alleged unbecoming conduct—instead of perceiving the women's refusal as an understandable reaction to a history of personally dealing with inappropriate behavior. Throughout my fieldwork, people often made direct generalizing references of others, usually unflattering comments about "all Haitians" or "all Dominicans" or "all foreigners" (meaning people from places other than Dominican Republic or Haiti).

And this was certainly not the only time during my fieldwork that I heard people call others by color and/or racial terms, as people referred to the women on the guagua as "negritas (little black women)" and "negras (black women)." In the Dominican Republic, it is customary to use descriptors as referents to get someone's attention when the first name for someone is unknown; these terms typically depict overt physical characteristics and include color and racial terms. For example, it is quite common for people to call out the terms *rubio* (blondie, and can refer to a person with light skin, regardless of hair color), *gordo* (fat), *gringo* (foreigner), *flaco* (skinny), as well as *blanco* (white or light skinned) or terms to connote darker skin, such as *moreno oscuro* or those terms used with the women on the bus. Dominicans sometimes use "negro/a" to refer to other Dominicans, and when they do so, it is often used as a term of endearment. However, when Dominicans use the term with Haitians, it has a negative connotation (Simmons 2009).

This chapter describes the multicultural community of Cabarete and the complexity of everyday interactions between and among people who live, work, and migrate there. The social construction of race in the Dominican Republic is, in part, a reflection of the long-standing tension developed over time through the history of colonialism, slavery, imperial intervention, and the movement of people to and from the island of Hispaniola. This tension manifests interpersonally among working-class Dominicans, Haitians, and Dominico-Haitians living in present-day La Cienaga and the Callejón, as it does for the entire Dominican Republic. But like only very few other regions of the Dominican Republic, such as some neighborhoods in Santo Domingo, life in Cabarete hinges upon consistent intercultural not intracultural engagement, paving the way for increased tension over resource allocation and belongingness and embodying what Anna Tsing (2005) calls friction: "[t]he awkward, unequal, unstable, and creative qualities of interconnection across difference." My discussion portrays common intercultural relations created out of the contemporary movement of ideas, symbols, beliefs, practices, and people who serve the tourism industry and demonstrates that in everyday encounters predicated on interpersonal engagement, Dominicans sometimes, but not always, use mechanisms of othering or practices that distinguish themselves as socially separate from, and superior to, Haitian/Dominico-Haitian residents.

To this end, I use examples of intercultural engagement throughout Cabarete in real and virtual ethnographic venues—the local Haitian church, the adult night school, a private language school, in international social media, and in places of employment—as sites where ideas, beliefs, and practices about racial/ethnic/national identity and belonging are negotiated and contested in Cabarete. Overall, intercultural engagement might indeed be determined by what Anna Tsing calls the "awkward, unequal, and unstable," since most people have experienced anti-Haitianism like Teresa and the two Kreyòl-speaking guagua passengers discussed in this chapter's opening story. But the contribution of this chapter, and the book overall, is to show the degree to which everyday life in Cabarete illustrates friction's "creative qualities of interconnection," meaning that in the Callejón and La Cienaga, race and nation are not the only or the primary constructs governing inter-cultural engagement. Instead, I argue that the lived experiences of people in La Cienaga and the Callejón show a much more complex picture of interconnection displayed in everyday interactions, including engagement in corner stores, the central venue which will be explored later in the book.

THE LEGACY OF ANTI-HAITIANISM
IN THE DOMINICAN REPUBLIC

Within an array of global processes, racial discourse in the Dominican Republic reflects a lasting legacy of the past in the present. Contemporary anti-Haitianism stems from the peculiarities of colonialism and slave-era miscegenation of European, Native American, and African populations on the island: a gradual process of French and Spanish colonialism, including overwork and mistreatment of local Taínos leading to their decimation and a lengthy and brutal African slave trade. The island was colonized under the Spanish crown in one of the first Columbus invasions in the late 1400s, exploiting indigenous people estimated to have numbered about 400,000 in 1492, in colonizers' search for gold. Within just twenty years, the indigenous population was depleted to less than 3,000. When "[b]oth the gold economy and the Indian population became extinct at the same time (Moya Pons 1998, 37)," the colonial administration of the whole island known as both Española and Santo Domingo imported African slaves to work in sugar plantations and in cattle ranching. By the early decades of the 1600s, the colony was divided by France and Spain: France claiming the western third of the island, called Saint-Domingue, and Spain administering the eastern two-thirds including the capital city of Santo Domingo. Although the island was to be unified again for brief periods of time over the next two centuries, this division set the stage for the two nations of the Dominican Republic and Haiti.

The colonial impacts on the island of Hispaniola resulted in a hierarchical system of racial categories centered on power and control. While a wealthy, land-owning elite of Spanish creoles—people of Spanish descent who were born on the island—held positions of authority within the colony, there were many other groups relegated to different rungs within the system, such as poor whites, freed people of color, and slaves. Working conditions on the island were not only brutal for Taínos, but also for slaves, and Santo Domingo had a difficult time reigning in rebellion because of it; most slaves were imported to the island, instead of being born there, due to high mortality rates brought about by overwork and disease (Moya Pons 1998). Slavery was outlawed in 1801 when Haiti became the second independent nation in the Western Hemisphere, but slavery persisted in the eastern half of the island until 1822. When rebellious slaves fled their oppressors and established their own communities, they created new racial terms to distinguish themselves from slaves and to emphasize their free status, such as *blancos de la tierra* (whites of the land) and *moreno oscuro* (dark brown), reserving the color term "black" for those who were still legally slaves (García-Peña 2015). These terms conflated whiteness with freedom and blackness with slavery, regardless of the actual skin color; in other words, this racial hierarchy represented a class-based system, reflecting people's position within the local economy.

Moreover, the period of Haitian colonization of the Dominican Republic from 1822 to 1844 further cemented conflations of blackness/otherness/Haitian and is often referred to as the starting point of tense Haitian-Dominican relations (Wynne 2014; Moya Pons 1998; Candelario 2007; Gregory 2014). In fact, Dominican Independence Day, annually celebrated on February 27, does not mark Dominican independence from Spain and its much longer period of colonialism on the island, but from Haiti, when the three founding fathers of the Republic, Juan Pablo Duarte, Ramón Matías Mella, and Francisco del Rosario Sánchez, declared war against their neighboring colonizers. García-Peña, in her book, *The Borders of Dominicanidad: Race, Nation, and Archives of Contradiction* (2016, 30), contends that "Hispanism and *mulataje* [literally, mulatto-ness, or notions of mixture based upon African and European descent] became the diction of revolution and mobilization against the unified Haitian government," meaning that the Dominican Republic signified Dominican identity with Spain and their mixed heritage against Haiti's links to slavery, Africa, and blackness. Using the case study of the deaths of three young girls and their father in a rural district of Santo Domingo called Galindo, at the hands of three self-identified "Spanish Dominicans," García-Peña (2016, 25) beautifully illustrates the origins of dominicanidad as that which is "not Haitian":

> Through a narrative of repetition, silencing, and exculpation . . . nineteenth-century Hispanophile writers—who privileged Spanish language, Hispanic culture, the traditions of Spain, and whiteness—memorialized Agueda, Ana Francisca, and Marcela Andújar [the girls] as white virgins and the first female martyrs of the nation . . . . Cobial, de la Cruz, and Gómez [the killers] in turn became bloodthirsty black Haitians . . . . This discursive strategy helped to sustain elite

desires for European cultural identity while appeasing global anxiety over the potential creation of another free black nation on the island of Hispaniola. Literature and History worked together in the production of Dominicanness in contrast to Haitianness; Galindo became one of the most important motifs for sustaining anti-Haitian ideology as the crime became a metaphor for the Haitian unification.

While Hispaniola had been home to two independent nations as early as 1804, for Haiti, and 1844, for Dominican Republic,[1] people regularly crossed the porous political border between the Dominican Republic and Haiti during the late nineteenth and early twentieth centuries, effectively establishing a bicultural region grounded in local trade (Wynne 2014; Moya Pons 1998; García-Peña 2015). The U.S. invasion of both nations on Hispaniola also affected the movement of people across the border. The U.S. marines occupied Haiti from 1915 to 1934 and the Dominican Republic from 1916 to 1924 under the auspices of protecting United States' interests. The U.S. occupation had economic, political, and cultural repercussions and implications on anti-Haitianism. At once, it concentrated the majority of agricultural lands in the hands of sugar plantations, almost all run by foreign-owned companies (Martínez 1999); it also established the *Guardia Nacional Dominicana* (the Dominican National Guard); and it ushered in an era of criminalizing Afro-religious figures and practices, such as leaders and adherents of *santería* or vodou or using sacred drums in religious services or festivals (García-Peña 2016). Most of the U.S. marines governing the island were white, so "[a]s white, civilized men, marines were charged with endowing people with civilization—whether that meant confiscating drums or killing prophets—even if the process required the use of uncivilized 'harshness'" (García-Peña 2016, 75).

In 1918, the Haitian constitution was rewritten, and in this process, an 1805 law was removed that criminalized foreign land ownership, setting the stage for increased American ownership of Haitian land and disenfranchising Haitian farmers. Toward the end of the 1920s, a bracero program had been established in the Dominican Republic to supply sugar plantations with cheap labor from Haiti, increasing the number of Haitians not only at the border, but throughout the country (Martínez 1996). This program also further linked the occupation of sugarcane cutting to Dominican representations of what it means to be Haitian and, therefore, black.

U.S. imperialism in Hispaniola paved the way for the rise of one of the most vicious dictators in Latin American and Caribbean history, Rafael Leónidas Trujillo Molina, since he enlisted in the Guardia Nacional in 1918 and worked closely with U.S. marines who were fostering anti-Haitianism. Trujillo's election in 1930 started the era known as the *trujillato* (Moya

Pons 1998; Simmons 2009). In public speeches, Trujillo would refer to the period of Haitian colonization of the Dominican Republic (1822–1844) as the "Haitian invasion" and use this to justify anti-Haitianist policies. Examples of anti-Haitianism during the trujillato included what is known colloquially as the 1937 Parsley Massacre[2], in which Trujillo ordered the slaughter of thousands of Haitians. He dispatched the military to the border and instructed soldiers to execute anyone found in the border town of Dajabón who had difficulty pronouncing the trilled "r" sound in the Spanish word for parsley, *perejil*. To reestablish international credibility after the massacre, Trujillo encouraged the immigration of European Jews during World War II, of which the motivating factor of this policy was to "whiten" the Dominican Republic—a process grounded in Dominican Jewish miscegenation (Torres-Saillant 2000). The irony is that while in Europe, Jews were not considered white, but in the Dominican Republic Jews were welcomed as desirable for being lighter skinned than most Dominicans (Simmons 2009). Wynne (2014, 154) contends that these events, among others, led to today's "stratified border relations" and the contemporary reproduction of anti-Haitianist ideology in the Dominican Republic. The Parsley Massacre is commemorated in Dajabón each year, and a mural has been painted there to depict the events (Bishop 2019; Bishop and Fernandez 2017).

Simmons (2008) describes the salience of anti-Haitianism in the trujillato and its links to what she calls the Dominican Republic's process of "burying the African past." For example, Trujillo ordered the rewriting of Dominican history textbooks to erase any mention of links to Africa, creating a whole generation of Dominicans who were kept in the dark about the contributions of African descendants to their own society. Simmons contends that instead of Dominicans denying their African heritage, they were systematically denied their past, which resulted in a Dominican imaginary of Africa and all things African as a referent for Haiti and Haitians.

Relocalized Social Constructions of Race and Other: From *De Color* to *La Sentencia*

The contemporary social construction of race in the Dominican Republic is rooted "in periods of emigration out of and immigration into the Dominican Republic, where ideas of race and culture were constantly re-formed with distance from blackness" (Simmons 2009, 21). Candelario (2007), Simmons (2009), García-Peña (2016), and Gregory (2014) demonstrate that racialized categories in the Dominican Republic have always been distinctions made in relation to others in a changing transnational landscape, where "relocalized" (Candelario 2007) ideas about race have been transported to the Dominican Republic, synthesized, and remade into racial/color terms that reflect syncretic racial meanings. While racial categories in the Dominican Republic pivot on a white/black divide, these colors also subsume more than just skin color; this divide includes not only phenotypes but also non-phenotypic factors, such as occupation, socioeconomic status, and nationality (Simmons 2009; Ricourt 2016).

Colloquial and scholarly renderings of Dominican racial discourse illustrate the variety of terms Dominicans use to distinguish race and national belonging and how they have changed over time. In fact, in the early 1900s, Dominican newspaper advertisements, often marketing beauty products, used the phrase *de color* (of color) to refer to people in the Dominican Republic; but by the 1930s, the phrase was rarely, if ever, used again (Simmons 2009). During the trujillato, the preferred color term *indio* (literally, Indian) was established to distinguish mixture as a race/color category. Although "indio" has never been used on the census, with *mestizo* (literally, mixed) used in its place, it has been estimated that a good majority of Dominicans are referred to as indio, sometimes up to 85% of the population using the term to self-identify. But the meaning of indio has nothing to do with the indigenous groups of the island who had been wiped out. Instead, Simmons (2009, 29) points out,

> [t]he construction of indio as a non-black, mixed, race/color category is in relation to Haitians, who were defined on the census as black . . . . Over time, the usage of indio color descriptors and categories had the effect of distancing Dominicans from their African heritage and ideas of blackness in an attempt to create an affinity toward Spanish against an indigenous (Taíno) landscape.

Thornton and Ubiera (2019, 417) further indicate that "[t]he local color term 'indio/a' gestures toward this mixed, neither-white-nor-black identity that Dominicans presumably share and which functions as a native category of Dominican creole identity."

In an online source called, "La Galería: Voices of the Dominican Diaspora," López (2019) explains that "the famous term, 'indio' . . . is actually quite a misunderstood term" and shows the degree to which indio is part of a system of Dominican historical "colorization" (Simmons 2008), a system of intragroup naming that shifts according to points of reference:

> In short, Dominicans do not use the term Indio to deny blackness but to more accurately describe a color which is not as light as white and not as dark as Moreno, although this largely depends on the person and there are huge overlaps between Indio and Moreno (it gets confusing). For example the use of Indio oscuro and Indio claro are very interesting, they depend entirely on the point of view of a person. For example, in a group of very pale people it is often said that

someone who is caramel/light brown will be Indio claro, to distinguish them,
even though to a group of dark-skinned people the light-brown subject will be
usually called "Blanco," and conversely Indio oscuro is often used by people
who are around darker people in that moment or have relatives who are darker
to distinguish him or herself from the others.

As he further explains the ethnographic usage of these terms, López makes
another important distinction: "These terms are never solid and not used as
an identifier, but rather a quick description of a person." In other words, it is
not Dominican to say, "I am an indio claro," in the same way that a person
from the United States might indicate that they are *an* African American or
a white person. Instead, these nonessentializing racial terms are fraught with
nuance and often change depending upon the context.

Corroborating my own experience leading a study abroad program in
the Dominican Republic with students from the United States, Simmons'
(2009) work shows that racial constructions in the Dominican Republic do
not align with the essentialized understanding of what it means to be black
for African Americans in the United States. For years, Simmons brought
American students abroad to the Dominican Republic, and she also directed
a study abroad organization in the Dominican Republic; these experiences
gave her numerous opportunities to hear from Americans of different ethnic
and racial backgrounds about the ways Dominicans categorized themselves
and Americans using Dominican racial discourse. African American students from the United States—a nation with a rule of hypodescent, where
black has been used to refer to people of mixed heritage since the 1920s—
were disheartened when Dominicans indicated that only those students with
the darkest skin might be considered black. In 2012, I brought ten students
from my university to the Dominican Republic: six white students, one
Honduran American student with white features, one Hmong-American
student, and two African American students (one student who self-identifies
as "Native Born Black," meaning that he was born in the United States and
other Americans consider him African American, and one student who was
born in Jamaica). Before we left for the Dominican Republic, one African
American student expressed concern that Dominicans might discriminate
against him because he might be considered Haitian, but this never happened. This student was unsettled when Dominicans failed to refer to him
as black: he was called, "gringo canela," a term emphasizing his foreign
status ("gringo") and his medium brown color, while the other African
American student was called "gringa morena," referring to her as a foreigner with darker skin. All of the students in the program were surprised,
in part, because these terms depicted African American students as outsid-
ers, even when, like Simmons' students, the African American students felt

some solidarity and "at home" in the Dominican Republic because, as they reported, "more people here look like me."

Constructing belonging in the Dominican Republic based upon ethno-racial-national lines has recently been further questioned and relocalized over the last two decades in two interesting and diametrically opposed ways—ways that allude to the conflicts that we see revolving around race, the nation, and belonging in the Dominican Republic. While Trujillo ushered in a category to conceptualize mixed heritage as "indio," a more recent racial discourse of *mulataje* (mulato-ness) has emerged in the Dominican Republic emphasizing mixture around an Afro-Latin identity (see Rahier (2003) and Whitten and Torres (1998) for examples of mulataje elsewhere in Latin America). Simmons (2009) describes the rise and fall of activist organizations in the early 2000s, such as the now defunct organizations called *Casa por la Identidad de las Mujeres Afro* (House of Women of African Identity) and *Café con Leche* (Coffee with Milk), working toward "unburying the African past" in the Dominican Republic. Recent activism celebrating Afro-Dominicanness has intersected with gender with regard to hair texture and style. Instead of upholding images of beauty that coincide with European hairstyles, such as chemically straightened long hair, activists such as Carolina Contreras, amicably known as Miss Rizos (Miss Curl in English), promote natural curly hairstyles in her salons in Santo Domingo and New York. Her work has led to online campaigns such as #yoamomipajon (*yo amo mi pajón* in English means, I love my natural curly hair), and Contreras has contended that reclaiming natural hair as beautiful is therapeutic for women who have been taught to hate their naturally curly hair (Leon 2015).

While this recent activism has centered on claiming and honoring African roots in the Dominican Republic, it has had little effect on re-envisioning anti-Haitianism. In other words, there has not been a shift in mainstream Dominican discourse that links Dominican and Haitian identities to their shared degrees of African heritage. One of the recent manifestations of anti-Haitianism has resulted in changes to long-standing immigration and citizenship policies in the Dominican Republic. Since 1929, the Dominican Republic has granted citizenship to all children born on Dominican soil to parents of Haitian heritage; this policy was established to attract migrant workers to work in the sugarcane fields of the Dominican Republic (Moya Pons 1998). But in 2013, *La Sentencia TC 0168–13* was upheld by the Supreme Court, effectively annulling citizenship to residents who were born to undocumented parents who live and work—often for their entire lives—in the Dominican Republic (Association of Black Anthropologists 2014; Petrozziello 2014). For all intents and purposes, although the ruling doesn't explicitly target Haitians, it especially affects those of Haitian heritage. Researchers have found that, in this social context, access to basic needs, such as health care, housing, jobs, and even the ability to freely travel on public transportation within the Dominican Republic, has become more and more difficult for Dominicans of Haitian heritage living in the Dominican Republic (Keys et al. 2015; Guzmán 2019). Along with increased militarization at the border of the Dominican Republic and Haiti, since the advent of La Sentencia, there are Dominican civic groups calling for erecting a border wall to control and decrease cross-border traffic (e.g., Dominican Today 2019). But organizations such as Reconoci.do and Centro Bonó have worked ardently to raise international awareness of the plight of statelessness among many people of Haitian heritage who were born in the Dominican Republic. Their work is integrated with those who shed light on the roots of African heritage in the Dominican Republic.

During my fieldwork, I witnessed examples of both overt and covert anti-Haitianism, as well as counter-hegemonic discourse from residents who were attempting to intentionally challenge racist stereotypes and discrimination in the Callejón and La Cienaga. The next section describes the neighborhoods of La Cienaga and the Callejón before turning to specific examples of friction encountered in typical intercultural engagement in Cabarete.

THE NEIGHBORHOODS OF CALLEJÓN DE LA LOMA AND LA CIENAGA

"*¡Ah, esa bulla! ¡Nunca me deja!*" (Oh, that racket! It never leaves me!) cried Belkis, rolling her eyes as we walked down the main street of the Callejón. And I couldn't agree with her more; the Callejón is a very noisy place, day and night, especially for a neighborhood of approximately 4,000 people. The cacophony of sounds comes from everywhere: motorcycle taxis, called *motoconchos*; loud music blaring from stereos in homes and bars; personal cars and taxis; groups of school children walking to and from school; itinerant food vendors, called *plataneros*, with their wheelbarrows full of plantains and bananas; food trucks, called *vendedores ambulantes* or *guaguas ambulantes*, calling out over their loudspeakers to advertise their produce for sale; the iconic bang of a domino hitting the card table while groups of people play in the shade of the afternoon siesta.

Located just south of Highway 5 within the downtown district of Cabarete, El Callejón de la Loma is accessible to most tourists who come to the area. The north side of Highway 5 lies on the coast, and most of the area's hotels, restaurants, bars, and nightclubs are located on this beach-front. Not a single guagua enters the Callejón, so residents walk the length of the neighborhood to Highway 5 to catch a ride to their destination. The one of the only paved roads in the Callejón is the *calle principal* (main

Figure 1.1   Food Truck in the Callejón. Photo taken by the author.

street) that begins at the highway and shoots straight through the neighborhood like an alley, ending 2 kilometers down the street at the entrance of El
Choco National Park, a small protected area of 75 square kilometers with
a few hiking trails, preserving some small limestone caves and the Lagoon
La Goleta, used as a swimming hole by local kids. Four kilometers west of
the entrance to the Callejón on Highway 5 lies La Cienaga, a much sleepier
neighborhood in comparison given that it is not within walking distance
of downtown Cabarete and most of the beachfront hotels, restaurants, and
other tourist businesses.

Both neighborhoods are set up similarly: they each have two entrances into the barrio that act as the main thoroughfares with various secondary, residential, and dead-end side streets radiating out like centimeter marks on a ruler. The Callejón side streets are pocked with mostly one-story cement-block homes that abut each other, with small, hastily constructed, one-room units built either on a second floor or squeezed into the small spaces between homes. La Cienaga has fewer residences with more open space between them; but like the Callejón, most of the homes are one-story cement-block structures with the occasional two-story, multiple-family dwelling. The Callejón's calle principal contains multiple speed bumps (*policía acostado*, which in Spanish literally means, "lying down police") as a way to slow down the flow of traffic, although motorcycles frequently race side by side down the main street, breaking sharply as soon as they near each speed bump. Main street in the Callejón is the location of most of the neighborhood's commercial district, such as corner stores, bars, restaurants, fruit stands, a combined computer repair store and internet café, and a couple of small secondhand clothing boutiques. It is also the site of the Catholic church, the Dominican Pentecostal church, and the public elementary and high schools attended by students from both the Callejón and La Cienaga. The plaza principal, or the neighborhood common area which is the site of Independence Day festivities for the whole town of Cabarete, consists of a paved basketball court and a one-story building serving as the city morgue and funeral parlor, and once or twice a year, this building becomes the site of the make-shift clinic for a medical mission from the United States, replete with dentistry, optometry, and primary health-care services. La Cienaga lacks any plaza principal or congested rows of businesses like that found in the Callejón. La Cienaga feels less urban than the Callejón; in fact, one of the defining features of La Cienaga is a centrally located, fenced-off field that serves as a grazing area for a few cows and goats belonging to a couple of neighborhood families, giving the community a decidedly rural atmosphere.

Because of the Callejón's proximity to the center of town and the beach-front hotels, this neighborhood attracts tourists and international residents. Conversely, residents of La Cienaga, people who sometimes interact directly with tourists in their workplaces, make it a matter of pride that their neighborhood is more private, slower paced, and away from the busyness of the Callejón. But the Callejón economically benefits from their location, something residents recognize, like Don José, a sixty-year-old fruit stand owner near the entrance to the Callejón: "I get a lot of pedestrians walking past the entrance [to the Callejón], so they see my store and come shop before heading to the beach, which is just across State Highway 5. I probably make a quarter—at least—of my profit from foreigners [tourists]." The entrance to the Callejón also has three upscale restaurants, establishments that serve international cuisine and are full bursting with tourists every weekend evening—so much so that late one Saturday night, a Dominican friend of mine from out of town took one look at the bustling entrance to the Callejón, turned to me with a look of surprise, and asked me, "Where are the Dominicans?"

Neither neighborhood is segregated, meaning that Dominicans, Haitians, and international residents live side by side in both locales. After mapping the neighborhoods and conducting a brief census of who lived there, I found that approximately 65% of residents in each neighborhood were Dominican, 34% were people of Haitian descent, and only 1% were international residents primarily from Europe, Canada, and the United States. The neighborhoods of the Callejón and La Cienaga, while ethnically diverse, are primarily homogeneous with regard to class. While it is rare for international residents to own property in these neighborhoods, most of the owner-occupied homes are Dominican; none of the homes are owned by people of Haitian descent. The majority of Haitians and Dominico-Haitians rent homes or apartments from Dominicans, and in just one known case, an absentee landlord from Quebec rents a home to a family of Haitian descent.

A handful of NGOs also reside in the Callejón that accommodate international volunteers in small houses scattered throughout the neighborhood. There are two additional area NGOs located in or near La Cienaga, and interestingly, their international volunteers also live in the Callejón, not La Cienaga, because of the inventory of small rental properties there. These are primarily short-term stays, so most volunteers stay for no more than a few months at a time and, outside of the volunteer work they contribute to the organization, do not become ensconced in the community. For the most part, the NGOs work with children in some capacity, so many of the neighborhood's children can often be seen calling out to international residents by name, while the volunteers often are unknown to most parents and other adults in the community. Adults sometimes treated volunteers with suspicion—not an irrational response, since sex tourism and child trafficking proliferate in the area. On two occasions during my fieldwork, I witnessed representatives from the *Departamento de Niñez, Adolecencia, y Familia* (Department of Childhood, Adolescence, and Family) detain an international male resident living in Cabarete under the suspicion that they were endangering local children.

Cabarete, and the north coast region overall, is especially vulnerable to food insecurity due to the high degree of migration, poverty, and international tourism. The rate of poverty in the region is grave, with 44.7% of all homes categorized as "poor." Additionally, 45% of people in the state of Puerto Plata are chronically malnourished (Oficina Nacional de Estadísticas 2016). Of the fifty working-class and poor Dominican and Haitian residents I interviewed, 40 of them (80%) had skipped a meal that day, with 100% of them declaring that they had skipped between four and six meals within the same week; the central motivating factors resulting in skipped meals were "not enough food" and "too busy/not enough time to cook and/or eat."

Most residents earn between 1,000 and 6,000 pesos a month, with a median monthly income of about 3,200 pesos. But a number of people reported making between 200 and 500 pesos a month, and some who, at certain times throughout the year, make almost nothing since they are not consistently employed, working at a marginal job within the local economic context of "just-in-time" capitalism (Nealon 2012). In other words, when there are no tourists, most of the working-class residents of El Callejón and La Cienaga have little work and, subsequently very little income. A typical example of this pattern was articulated by Neida, a nineteen-year-old Dominican from Santo Domingo who has been living with her cousins in Cabarete since she was fifteen and works as a maid in a local five-star hotel in downtown Cabarete. As one of the youngest and most recently hired maids, she is the first person laid off from her job when the tourist season slows down in mid- to late September. "Frankly, from September until the beginning of December I have no shifts at work. . . . Then, I don't work much between Carnaval [usually sometime in early February] and Semana Santa [the week leading up to Easter]. I have no savings to use during these times, so my household has less money to buy what we need. We skip meals a lot during these months."

Residents who work providing services on the beach are hit especially hard when tourism slows down. Simone, a twenty-six-year-old Dominico-Haitian who has lived in Cabarete with her husband and three young children for five years, earned her license as a masseuse in Sosúa four years ago and has been working as an ambulant masseuse on Cabarete beaches ever since. Each day, she walks up and down the beaches asking tourists if they'd like to pay her for a timed massage. On any given day during the high tourist season, she can earn up to 2,000 pesos for an eight-hour workday. But "these are not earnings that I can count on year-round," she told me. Even when area hotels might be busy during Carnaval or Semana Santa, Simone explains that "this doesn't mean that the tourists are lying on the beach on vacation. No, often the hotels are full of Dominicans or foreign tourists who are here to go to Carnaval in La Vega (the most popular destination in the Dominican Republic for Carnaval, located in the center of the country about 50km from Cabarete), so they're not here for the beach. This means if I walk the beaches during this time, I earn no money." Santos, a thirty-seven-year-old resident of La Cienaga who migrated from a rural community near Cap Hatien, Haiti, walks the beach every day with a plastic tub on his head, out of which he sells homemade peanut-brittle candies his wife prepares in the early hours of each morning. He repeated the same refrain I heard many times from others who live in the Callejón and La

Cienaga: "I earn no money in the slow season . . . it's come to the point that my wife doesn't even get up to make the candies because she knows we won't even afford the ingredients to make them."

Even residents who provide more skilled services in the local tourist industry, such as Josef, a twenty-four-year-old Dominican kite-surfing instructor, suffer during these lean months. This area of the north coast is known for its windy days and warm waters, excellent conditions for sport enthusiasts who strap a board to their feet and a narrow parachute to their backs, which they use to guide them through the waves along the Cabarete shoreline. In fact, every July, Cabarete hosts one of the biggest kite-surfing festivals in the world. Josef speaks three languages, English, German, and Spanish, making him marketable in a service economy attracting international tourists. During the summer months, he can sometimes take out as many as three groups of tourists a day to teach them the basics of kite-surfing through a local kite-surfing school. But working as an instructor is a fickle job: "Usually, I can rely on my instructor income during the summer months and sometimes Christmas [meaning about a month between mid-December and mid-January]. But I don't make enough to live here [in the Callejón] any other time of the year. There's just not enough work, so they don't call me in to work." Josef and his wife, Aledia, operate a small, financially struggling colmado in La Cienaga, where Aledia runs the day-to-day operations and Josef works there whenever he is not teaching. When Josef is available in their colmado, Aledia cooks homemade stewed pinto beans (*habichuelas*) to sell in bags at their own colmado, and she and her two neighbors travel to the Callejón and are allowed to sell the bags at colmados throughout the Callejón.

While colmados were the primary sites of my research, my work in other venues allowed me to compare and contrast the variety of intercultural relations in Cabarete. I conducted participant observation in the following community venues where residents of the Callejón and La Cienaga spend their time: a Haitian church; two NGOs; a private language school catering to neighborhood adults, who have enrolled to build their marketability by learning conversation skills in other languages; and the adult night school program, called the *escuela básica*, for students to complete their high school diploma equivalency. My participant observation in these venues also revealed the relevance of international networks people connect with via social media to how they interpret and understand everyday intercultural encounters in Cabarete. Additionally, I carried out twenty ethnographic interviews and two focus groups with both Dominicans and Haitians who work, volunteer, or participate in these community venues; most of them live in the Callejón and La Cienaga, while a few of them do not. My fieldwork in these venues revealed that anti-Haitianism persists in everyday life in Cabarete, but there are orchestrated, on-the-ground advancements being made to promote cooperative and productive interactions between Dominicans and people of Haitian descent. Below, I use specific examples from these sites to give a range of people's reactions to intercultural engagement, demonstrating the resulting friction that reproduces some tension but also produces honest dialogue and understanding.

ARTICULATING INCLUSION AND EXCLUSION IN CABARETE

The Haitian Church

The Callejón is home to one Haitian Christian church, located on a side street within the neighborhood. Its members come from La Cienaga and the Callejón, with a few members who live as far away as Sosúa. Weekly Sunday services hold between forty-five and sixty people. The church is also used as a common meeting room for church members, so I would often be invited to interview people at the church instead of at their houses. Every night of the week there are Bible studies, women's groups, choir practice, and children's activities such as rehearsals for a girls' dance troupe. It is a busy place and the church members are very involved; many members reported that the church was a second home for them because they spent so much time there, sometimes more time in the church than in their own homes.

The church also served as a gathering place to discuss problems affecting the local community. On February 28, 2015, instead of having the usual Bible study, church members met to discuss events in the Dominican Republic surrounding the vigilante hanging of a Haitian man in Santiago and deportations at the border (see Santana 2015). About thirty-five church members met during this hour to discuss how to protect themselves if anti-Haitian violence were to occur in Cabarete. Many people talked about how afraid they had become, especially after one member told everyone at the meeting about something he had seen watching the news at a nearby corner store with other residents, both Dominican and Haitian: that then-president Danilo had announced on television that he would wage war against Haiti. The church discussion revolved around other specific events that had been featured in the news, such as the recent mass burning of the Dominican flag in Haiti, a reciprocal mass burning of the Haitian flag in the Dominican Republic, and increased deportations in Dajabón at the northern border crossing of the Dominican Republic and Haiti. After the meeting was over, one of the members approached me to tell me that he was going to send his wife back to her family's house in a small community outside of Jimaní, on the southern border. "I'm too scared for her," he said of his wife. "She doesn't speak any

Spanish and she has just had an operation, so if she had to flee for her life, she couldn't do it. I think it might be best if she goes back to Haiti."

Sunday services are led by a Haitian pastor, who during the week lives in Ouanaminthe, Haiti, a border community 212 kilometers west of Cabarete near the Dominican town of Dajabón, and travels each weekend to Cabarete, making the journey that can last more than four hours with border crossings. Church services are filled with live music, singing, reading from the Bible, and call and response prayers. The last forty minutes of each Sunday service are reserved for the pastor's message. These messages are not only commentaries on the Bible passages that are read that day but also reflections on contemporary events. On Sunday, March 1, 2015, the pastor specifically addressed his congregation's fears and issues that had been discussed at the earlier meeting. "Don't be afraid. When you fear, you act from that fear and provoke more fear. If people you know talk about these events with fear, walk away. Go inside your home. Don't say yes, we should leave. There will be no war. No one wants a war. The whole world is watching us; the international community will not allow a war between our nations. Do not fear." This message helped ease some tension in the minds of his congregants. He went on to say:

> Our message, our objective should not be to break relations with the Dominican Republic. This will hardly do us any good. We work here, we have families here, and we have families in Haiti. Rather, I'm looking for harmony, solidarity, respect for both peoples, because we are all poor here in the Callejón. I don't want one country on the island of Hispaniola. No, I want us to have real dialogue and respect for our differences . . . you know, we [Dominicans and Haitians] both are needed here!

In his sermons and in interviews with me, the pastor was careful to avoid referring to unity between the nations of the Dominican Republic and Haiti. Instead, his words supported the neo-Marxist position of strengthening solidarity in the neighborhood between and among workers who filled an exploited economic niche in the local tourism industry.

Wilman, a thirty-five-year-old Haitian who moved to the Callejón in 2009, appreciated his pastor's perspective and endeavored to do more. He founded a men's choral group called *Gwoup Resistanz* (Resistance Group, in Kreyòl) and scheduled concerts three times a year, inviting residents of the Callejón and La Cienaga, members of the local Dominican Pentecostal church, as well as international residents and tourists who reside at the apartment complexes where he works in another Cabarete neighborhood. Most of the performances included gospel songs sung in Kreyòl, but they often included one or two songs sung in Spanish on the program, "to show that we do learn the national language of Dominican Republic, our adopted home," he told me. International residents are required to buy tickets to the concerts to raise money for the church and the choral group, but local residents from the neighborhoods, including members of the Dominican Pentecostal church, were allowed in for free. I attended three performances of Gwoup Resistanz, and each concert was attended by about twenty international residents/tourists and twenty members of the church and other people from the neighborhoods. No members of the Dominican Pentecostal church were in attendance. When I asked Wilman about the absence of Dominican Christians to whom he had extended a personal invitation, Wilman said he wasn't surprised because "change is slow. We are going to continue to invite them, and we'll see if they come. I want us all to see that there is more between us that's similar than different." What are some similarities between Dominicans and Haitians, I asked him to explain to me? "Well, in Cabarete, we are all poor, we all work hard here to give others a good time on holiday. If it weren't for Haitians and Dominicans in the Callejón, nobody would come here [to vacation]."

But not everyone agreed with Wilman. Another member of Gwoup Resistanz named Didi, who had moved to the Callejón within the last year, vehemently opposed the decision to invite members of the Dominican Pentecostal church to their concerts. Didi was a current member of a construction crew responsible for repairing the roof of a home in the nearby town of Sabaneta de Yásica. One of his crewmates was a member of the Dominican church, and he had single-handedly given Didi a hard time at work since the start of the project. "My Spanish is growing, but I don't understand everything that is said all the time. But I know when he's talking badly about me. I'm not the only Haitian on the crew, but I'm the only one who has moved here [to Cabarete] within the last year. One time he grabbed my cell phone and started to dial, tried to use up my minutes [on the phone card Didi had bought], and I had to grab it back. He just laughed." Didi went further to explain that he is satisfied that none of the members of the Dominican church have ever taken them up on the invitation to attend a performance. Didi reported that if he had seen one of the members of the church, especially his ill-mannered crewmate, he doesn't know what he would do. "All Dominicans are like him," Didi exclaimed. "They're all lazy dogs. They steal right from our hands."

International Networks

Residents in the Callejón are well aware of national manifestations of anti-Haitianism. And these events are fodder not only to inform but to point to ways to challenge friction and improve intercultural interactions. For example, at 8:00 p.m. on February 25, 2015, I entered Rita's house on Calle

8 to find twelve people all standing around a cell phone watching a video. When I inquired about what was going on, I was told, politely but firmly, to shut up and sit down. Michelín, who owned the cell phone, waited until the video ended and then brought it over to me. Even though they had already seen it, about nine people in the crowd came over to where I was sitting and watched the video again with me. I was appalled by what I saw: a man speaking Kreyol was tied at his wrists and his ankles and was lying down on the ground. Five men who spoke Spanish were standing around him with large wooden sticks in their hands. Everyone was yelling, and then the man on the ground was hit repeatedly by the men with sticks. At one point, one of the attackers said, let's call the police and have them deal with him, referring to the man on the ground. The video ended in mid-beating with the man still tied up.

When the video was over, people did not say much but found a place to sit down. I asked Michelín where she got the video, and she said her boyfriend in New York sent it to her, warning her to be careful or preferably to leave the country and go back to Haiti. "What are you going to do?" I asked. She said nothing, except, "I'm glad he sent it to me." I ventured further: "Where did that video take place?" She said she didn't know, but she suspected Dominican Republic because of the perpetrators' accents, the tropical environment, and the fashion of the clothes worn by everyone in the video. Again, she repeated that she was glad her boyfriend sent it to her. "We have to tell others about these things and share them with others, so they know," she told me. "Do you think this is common, or something that will happen here?" I asked. Everyone said, "No, this isn't common, and no, we don't think it will happen here." "But who knows?" replied Jonás.

Other residents reported using social media sites not only to stay informed but also to become involved in social change. Like Michelín, Robens shares information about contemporary events and politics in the Dominican Republic with others, mostly through his Facebook site. Robens was born in Cabarete to Haitian migrants, which legally made him a Dominican citizen until Ley 0168–14 was passed that forced him to regularize his status after his citizenship had been stripped by the 0168–13 Constitutional Ruling. He actively seeks out news and posts activities from international and national organizations, such as Reconoci.do, *Dominicanos por Derechos Humanos* (Dominicans for Human Rights), Centro Bonó, and Amnesty International. His international social network includes friends and family from Haiti, Dominican Republic, the United States, and England. Of his use of social media, he says:

Sometimes, I find out about things going on here from friends in New York. Sometimes, I post news first to others. But I first found out about the 2014 Law from an organization in Santo Domingo . . . I can't remember which one. I post to inform about the Dominican way [*le dominicaine*] that has been hurting Haitians, but I use my contacts to help people here in the Callejón. I was born here—I want to stay here. But I don't know if this is the place for me. Who am I? Where do I fit in here? Keeping in contact with people in this way helps me feel a little bit more like I belong here.

Residents of Cabarete cast a wide net: they use international social networks not only to inform themselves of current events, but to challenge local perceptions inasmuch as it makes and remakes "the images of the world created by these media" (Appadurai 1996, 9; Appadurai 1990). In other words, Michelín's and Robens' use and understanding of the messages they receive in these media is part of a social process. The stories of Michelín and Robens demonstrate the ways that people in the Callejón use media to help them have a better sense of their place in Cabarete—both to feel a sense of belonging, like Robens, and to be aware of potential threats, like Michelín.

Adult Night School

Solidarity and respect for differences were topics discussed with students in adult basic education classes. In the Dominican Republic, these classes are comparable to alternative diploma or GED programs in the United States, whereby students who have dropped out of formal classes attend night school to obtain an equivalent high school diploma. In Cabarete, Haitians often attend these classes not to obtain an equivalent diploma, but to learn Spanish, even though their classes are in mathematics, reading, and writing, not Spanish language instruction. These classes are free to those who enroll, and in my interviews, many Dominicans referred to these free classes as evidence of the Dominican government's generosity to Haitians living and working within its borders. Other foreign workers, such as those from Western Europe or Canada, were not eligible to register for adult education classes and were referred to one of the area's two private language schools to learn Spanish for a fee. Many Dominicans in the Callejón pointed out that the benefit of using free adult night class to learn Spanish that is in practice was only afforded to Haitians was a "gift," as Oscar, a nineteen-year-old Dominican who stopped going to high school when he was fourteen, articulated in conversations with me.

Only Haitians come to night school to learn Spanish. I don't see any tourists there from other countries . . . who might really want to learn Spanish. No, for them, they go to [a local private language school], which is costly. Only Haitians get this gift. I have a friend from Norway here, he's about 20, and doesn't have a lot of money. I told him about these night school classes, and he showed up one night, but they wouldn't let him in . . . at least, he thinks they wouldn't let him in [laughs]. . . . His Spanish is awful! No, I asked around for him and everyone says that he can't attend because he should go to [the private school].

During my fieldwork, I accompanied Rosaly, a Haitian migrant who had resided in the Dominican Republic only five months at the time, to adult basic education classes. Her teachers gave me permission to accompany Rosaly so that I could help her practice the Spanish she learned in class. One night before the teacher had arrived, a new student entered the class, one who we had never seen before. Rosaly and I were speaking Kreyòl to each other, laughing and joking before class started. The new student, a boy of about fourteen, looked right at Rosaly and commanded, "You must speak Spanish!" Rosaly said in Kreyòl, "That's why I'm here," and I translated this to the boy, who had no further comments.

During class that evening, the professor, a Dominican woman who had been teaching for fourteen years, had students take turns reading a passage out of a reader about tolerance and respect for all people. The teacher engaged the students in a discussion of what tolerance and respect for differences mean. Student responses ranged from "not making fun of people," to "learning Spanish since they are in our country." The teacher summed up the conversation: "Our country succeeds when we give respect to others even when they're different from us. She speaks Kreyòl (pointing at Rosaly), she speaks English (pointing at me), we speak Spanish, but we're all living here now. The [government of] Dominican Republic prioritizes this. . . . They are paying for her schooling [points to Rosaly]." This final point, allowing Haitians access to adult night schooling, was an important comment that signaled institutional support of the migrant experience.

On our walk home from class that evening, Rosaly commented on the lesson and put it in context:

> Respect is something that is taught but not given in Cabarete. Pastor says that we [Dominicans and Haitians] are all in this together, meaning that we all contribute something when we work here. I'm able to speak French with tourists . . .. Dominicans don't do that! I help bring tourists here and make them feel comfortable, and then they go eat at a restaurant, and stay in a hotel room, and do other things . . . things that they spend money on. This helps us all here! [CH: Have you seen more respect here over time?] Yes, we have found it to get better and better as we live here. But it's too slow for me . . .. Well, I haven't been here that long. I want words [like the boy's comment in class that night] to stop . . . but I am glad to take [free] classes to help my Spanish.

Workplaces

Cabarete's tourist economy requires the skills and talents of a diverse work-force, workers who speak a variety of languages and have the capacity to understand and relate to others unlike themselves. These contexts are ripe for the manifestation of friction about who belongs and who gets to belong. For example, Robe, who identifies as Dominico-Haitian and has lived in La Cienaga for over a decade, told me about a particular incident that offended him at work that specifically refers to his identity. Robe works for an NGO in the Callejón after having moved here from Santo Domingo where he was born and raised. One day at work, one of his coworkers told him that he is Haitian because he was born to Haitian parents. "This offended me," said Robe,

> not because I'm afraid of being Haitian. The Haitian way predominates in me (*Lo haitiano me predomina*). But because this statement rejects me even though I belong here. I have a Dominican identity card. I've been thinking that I may have to get a Haitian passport because of [the recent change in citizenship requirements]. But I belong here.

I asked him how he reacted when his colleague said this to him. He told me that he used this as an opportunity to teach him about his legal citizenship. He said that, in the end, his colleague told him that he did not mean to offend him, and he was just kidding, so Robe has no hard feelings about the incident. But he said this is one of many similar conversations that he has not only with Dominicans but also with tourists who hear his Kreyòl-inflected Spanish and assume he is Haitian.

Private Language School

Pedro, a fifty-year-old Dominican from the central city of La Vega, owned a private language school in the Callejón where students took English and German classes for a small fee. These night classes were held in a local private Christian elementary school, the principal of which was Pedro's wife, a woman who was born and raised in the Callejón. I conducted two focus groups with volunteers from Pedro's English classes, from the most basic English to advanced. Most of the students were enrolled in these classes to help them secure jobs working with tourists in Cabarete shops and organizations. For example, Luna, a twenty-six-year-old mother of two children who worked as a maid in a nearby hotel, hoped to gain employment in a local adventure tour agency. "I hate cleaning rooms, doing laundry [in her current job] . . . I could do so much more. I'm good with people, and I know Cabarete well. I want to help tourists see all of Cabarete, and I need to speak more than Spanish to do this."

Pedro, the only instructor at the language school, is a polyglot who loves learning and using languages. He speaks four fluently: Spanish, English, German, and French and studies Italian and Portuguese in his spare time. I asked him why he didn't teach French classes, since there are a large number of snowbirds from Quebec, international residents who live in Cabarete from December through May each year to escape their harsh winters. "Well," replied Pedro, "most Dominicans don't want to learn French because there are Haitians here who can do so more easily [than Dominicans]." This point was also corroborated by students in my focus groups. When asked why they don't take French, students echoed Oscar, who told me, "when a French-speaking foreigner needs help [in Cabarete], they seek out a Haitian. Haitians already speak French, so we [Dominicans] don't need to." This is not entirely true; there are Haitians in Cabarete who speak French fluently and can communicate with French-speaking residents and tourists, but many Haitians only speak Kreyòl and are not able to effectively communicate with Quebecois residents. To push the conversation further, I asked focus group participants why they didn't learn Kreyòl. In both focus groups, I got quiet stares in response to this question. When I asked Pedro why he didn't learn Kreyòl in his spare time, since so many Kreyòl speakers lived in Cabarete, certainly more Kreyòl speakers than Italian and Portuguese speakers, the two languages in which he was self-taught, he replied: "Cristina, there is no need to learn Kreyòl because we [the Dominican Republic] are trying to send them back to Haiti. There is no need for us to learn Kreyòl because Haitians are not tourists around here. Kreyòl doesn't help someone get a job around here."

CONCLUSIONS

This chapter illustrates the historical development of anti-Haitianism in the Dominican Republic and how it feeds back upon people's perceptions of and interactions with the Other in the Callejón and La Cienaga. Everyday life in Cabarete is typified by intercultural engagement, creating the conditions ripe for friction between different people. But contrary to the logic of the fatal-conflict model that assumes strained, negative, or domineering Haitian-Dominican interpersonal relations, these ethnographic examples highlight the complexity of Dominican-Haitian relations. Results in Cabarete demonstrate the nuances of contemporary anti-Haitianism and its effects on interactions between and among Haitians and Dominicans. While anti-Haitianism is an ever-present narrative, sometimes leading to antagonism and tension between people, everyday life requires people to engage in intercultural social networks and negotiate citizenship and their own identities among people residing in Cabarete and to others from abroad. Moreover, the fact that Haitians and Dominicans speak different languages, both of which are useful to local employers in the tourism industry, might decrease some of the stress between people and perhaps mitigate the stiff competition that could result as rivals in a scarce market economy. Anti-Haitian narratives are sometimes invoked in everyday engagement—whether at the church pulpit during a pastor's sermon or between people at work or in an adult night school or language classes—but sometimes intercultural interactions work against these narratives. In the process of intercultural engagement, sometimes people appeal to other factors, such as people's shared position on the lowest rungs in the tourism industry as Wilman did in Gwoup Resistanz, consequently undermining long-standing explanations and expectations of Dominican Haitian relations with surprising optimism.

The complexity of intercultural relations in Cabarete also extends to interactions in another important and ubiquitous Dominican venue, the colmado. In fact, Dominicans and Haitians frequent colmados and engage in intercultural interaction in colmados more than any other venue discussed in this chapter. Yet, this has not resulted in more anti-Haitianism; indeed, buying food using in-store credit in colmados has generated new intercultural networks that have helped many households garner resource they need to survive. The next chapter describes corner stores and the socioeconomic norms that govern food shopping in colmados.

NOTES

1. Dominican Republic briefly had a period of Spanish recolonization between 1861 and 1865. See Moya Pons (1998).

2. Derby (1994) offers an important revision of these events. Her essay points out that what is often referred to as the Haitian Massacre is misnamed because most of those who were slaughtered were Dominicans of Haitian heritage. Her essay indicates that it should be more aptly named, *El Masacre* (The Massacre), or *Kout Kouto*. She also questions the relevance of the litmus test referred to in many common accounts of the massacre, in which soldiers used the pronunciation of the word, parsley, to unveil people of Haitian descent.

Chapter 2

"Everything Is Cheaper at the Supermarket, but I Can't Afford It"

Colmados as a Total Social Phenomenon

30 June 2013

At 9:45 a.m., Esther and I had just walked out of the Haitian church where she was directing the girls' dance troupe to prepare for the upcoming community-wide church concert. As we walked from the church on 8th Street and made our way down Main Street, Esther, almost thinking out loud, said off-handedly that she needed to buy rice for that day. We walked into what was a new colmado for me, one that I had noted on my many walks down that street, observing the painted, scripted sign on the wall near the front entrance that said "Colmado Junior." Today, Junior was working behind the counter, and the nine customers waiting to be served bantered good-naturedly back and forth with Junior as well as with each other. Esther did not engage in small talk with other customers, but did call out to Junior when she arrived, exclaiming, "I'm back again, Junior!" Esther and I waited almost in total silence until Junior looked at Esther, signaling he was ready to take her order and calling to her with, "Y dime, morena (tell me, Black woman)." Esther asked for 20 pesos of rice, a small packet of cinnamon, and a can of Carnation evaporated milk. She asked for the notebook (cuaderno), and Junior sent her over to an adolescent boy who was inscribing the amount spent for purchases that would be paid for at a later date. Junior told the boy that she owed 70 pesos (approximately US$1.65), Esther nodded her agreement, and the boy repeated the total amount twice before writing it down on a page labeled with her name and a long row of crossed-out figures on the left-hand side of her designated space. Esther, satisfied that the written sum matched what she owed, walked out of the corner store with me in tow.

"Esther," I started as we continued walking to her home to make lunch, "you told me that you do most of your shopping in colmados, both here [in the Callejón] and in La Cienaga, but do you ever shop at the big supermarket?"

57

"You mean Janet's . . . No, I rarely go to Janet's . . . sometimes I might go with [her friend] Michelín, but I don't buy anything when I go in there."

"How come?" I asked. "I was in there the other day, and you can buy the same rice there in bigger bags. The tags on the shelves indicate the prices, and you can buy a big bag of rice there for less money than you would for the 20 peso-bags of rice you buy in the colmado."

"Yeah, of course, you're right, Cristina," Esther replied. "Everything is cheaper in the supermarket, colmados are more expensive, for sure. But shopping in the supermarket? I can't afford it [pero no me lo puedo permitir]."

Colmados are an important component in the foodscape of Cabarete. This chapter highlights the many reasons why colmados are the preferred shopping venue for all working poor and lower-class residents of El Callejón and La Cienaga. It also provides an explanation about the disconnect Esther refers to in our conversation in the fieldnotes above: shopping in colmados is more expensive than buying food from the big-box supermarket, but working poor residents of Cabarete cannot afford to shop in supermarkets and prefer colmados. The story of food shopping in colmados in Cabarete also is intertwined with the story of food shopping—or, what is more likely, not shopping—in supermarkets: in fact, every one of my interviewees in Cabarete discussed their reasons for shopping in colmados while simultaneously explaining why they so infrequently and irregularly shop in the one large, big-box style supermarket in Cabarete called Janet's. Colmados serve a number of important economic functions that supermarkets are not able to fulfill: colmados are conveniently located within their communities, shopkeepers attend to their customers' needs around the clock, and customers have the ability to purchase small amounts of essential food stuffs and prepared foods. All of these are unique characteristics of shopping in colmados and some important economic reasons for the preference of shopping in colmados for working poor residents in Cabarete. Quite simply, working poor residents of the Callejón and La Cienaga are able to eat because of colmados.

But it would be a mistake to distill residents' preferences for shopping in colmados solely for its economic benefits. This chapter also provides an ethnographic grounding of food shopping in Cabarete, paying particular attention to the ways colmados have become a "total social phenomenon," Krohn-Hansen's (2016) reference to Mauss' notion of total social facts (1966) which weave together and organize seemingly disparate spheres of social reality:

The processes and relationships that give the colmado its characteristic shape should not be reduced to mere economics. They also have cultural, affective, aesthetic, recreational, and political components. The typical colmado is a site for production and sustenance of forms of kinship and gender—and of relationships between friends and neighbors. It is also an arena for the experience of *lo criollo*, or of what it means to be Dominican, in landscapes shot through with marked and growing globalization and transnationalism . . . . [I]t continues to be massively and conspicuously present in Dominican society. (Krohn-Hansen 2016, 2)

Like results gleaned by Krohn-Hansen, residents of El Callejón and La Cienaga in my own research also referred to shopping in colmados for its affective, recreational, aesthetic, and cultural components, particularly as a space well known for its linkages to lo criollo, its identification with authentic, real, "homegrown" (Derby 1998) food, in a way that supermarkets do not. This chapter demonstrates that residents' conceptions of colmados integrate notions of that which is familiar as lo criollo, and colmados are vital for provisioning households with homegrown food. All shoppers, regardless of heritage—both Haitians and Dominicans alike—prefer shopping in colmados to buy homegrown food. Interviewees do not specifically refer to lo criollo as "what it means to be Dominican," as suggested in Krohn-Hansen's work; instead, both Haitians and Dominicans use this distinction to refer to food that is desirable, preferable, and recognizable, that which is set apart from supermarkets with too many options and its diversity of imported, unrecognizable foods.

Moreover, my research reveals that shopping in colmados is indeed a practice embedded within structures of kinship and gender. But results in Cabarete diverge in important ways from findings in other scholarship on colmados (e.g., Krohn-Hansen 2013; Murray 1996). In working poor neighborhoods in Cabarete, women do indeed provision households, and in so doing, frequent colmados more often than men and children—but just barely. Patrons of colmados include women, men, and children at distinct times of the day, and women often work and own colmados. Using gender and kinship as lenses to understand social and economic dynamics in colmados uncovers a complex system of local labor—people working in their roles as shoppers, shopkeepers, and delivery staff—that is imbued with power and meaning for *who* they are and as *how* and *when* they labor in colmados.

THE RISE OF COLMADOS IN THE DOMINICAN REPUBLIC

In the mid-1990s, there was a concerted effort in the Dominican Republic to bring together both Dominican and international quantitative and qualitative researchers to better understand the role and contribution of colmados within the Dominican economy and labor market. Ethnographic and survey analyses were supported through *El Fondo para el Financimiento de la Microempresa, Inc.*, a private think-tank referred to by the abbreviation FondoMicro, at a time when the Dominican economy saw a countrywide surge in micro-enterprises (*microempresas*), defined as businesses that employ fewer than ten employees (Murray 1996). Figures from FondoMicro studies validated both the ubiquity of colmados in the Dominican Republic—a phenomenon maintained through the present day—as well as the social, cultural, and economic relevance of colmados to both Dominican food shopping and entrepreneurial work. For example, Aristy Escuder (1995) found that one out of every four Dominicans working in micro-enterprises in the early 1990s were aspiring colmaderos, the majority stating that a major benefit of working as a colmadero was the promise of a steady income instead of working in seasonal jobs that ebb and flow with the tourist seasons.

Derby (1998) provides an historical perspective on the rise of this aspiration and shows how it is linked to the nation's history of sugar plantations and the transnational sugar industry. By the early twentieth century, the primarily foreign-owned sugar industry dominated the Dominican economy and was one of the chief sources of low-paying jobs in the Dominican Republic. Sugar, as an export crop, was grown on large, monocultural plantations and

Figure 2.1   A Shopkeeper Attending a Customer in La Cienaga. Photo taken by the author.

became synonymous with *lo extranjero* (the foreign). But in practical terms, the augmentation of sugar plantations throughout the country stripped poor, rural, peasant-wage workers of their hunting grounds in the *montes* (the countryside or bush). To explain the origin of shopkeeper as an entrenched and desirable economic profession in the Dominican Republic, Derby (1998, 464) shows that the industrialization of sugar affected local small-scale subsistence patterns, often leaving people with few other options:

> The monte was where the peasantry grew its garden vegetables, hunted for wild boars, and ranged unfenced cattle: thus it represented the security of an assured food supply outside the sphere of market exchange. The cutting of the monte was the closing of the Dominican frontier, and it left no alternative to becoming a vendor in a plantation bodega, a colmado (corner grocer), or a *colono* [sugar plantation worker].

By the middle of the twentieth century, the loss of hunting and grazing grounds resulted in a burgeoning micro-enterprise class of shopkeepers.

By the mid-1990s, approximately 45% of all Dominican micro-enterprises—144,217 out of all of the almost 320,000 total micro-enterprises—were involved with food, including establishments which sell foodstuffs and prepared foods, such as supermarkets, colmados, restaurants, bakeries, outdoor market stalls, as well as small food production companies, such as coffee roasters and candy factories (Moya Pons and Ortíz 1994). This figure also includes ambulatory food vendors who walk through neighborhoods selling food out of a wheelbarrow and are known for their unique sing-song-like calls to advertise their products to attract customers, and food sellers in pickup trucks who use a megaphone to announce their arrival and advertise their wares. At the time of this survey, almost half of all food micro-enterprises—approximately 72,000 of the ~145,000 micro-enterprises—were colmados (40,347) or *pulperías/ventorrillos* (31,754). This is a distinction that was not recognized during my fieldwork: in my research twenty years after this survey, I never heard the term pulpería used in the Dominican Republic. Further, in only a hand full of cases did I ever hear the word "ventorrillos," and it was never uttered in Cabarete. While colmados refer to corner stores into which customers enter via a door, ventorrillos refer to corner stores with walk-up windows where customers request to buy items from the shop owner. But in Cabarete, everyone who spoke with me about their food shopping referred to all corner stores—both walk-up window stores as well as those that are entered through a door—as colmados.

Murray conducted ethnographic fieldwork in two colmados in the capital city of Santo Domingo (1996) and published his findings in the book *El Colmado: Una Exploración Antropológica del Negocio de Comidas y*

Figure 2.2   A Typical Colmado in which Customers Are Served at a Walk-up Window.
Photo taken by the author.

Bebidas en la República Dominicana (The Corner Store: An Anthropological Exploration of the Sale of Food and Beverages in the Dominican Republic). This book was financed and published by FondoMicro as a complement to national-level quantitative surveys on Dominican food establishments. As such, *El Colmado* was the first in-depth scholarly study of (1) the factors that propel Dominicans to pursue working in and eventually owning a colmado and (2) the inner workings of opening and operating a colmado. Murray explains that the development of colmados in the Dominican Republic is intertwined with the history of the growth of urban cities, starting in the 1950s and increasing throughout the latter half of the twentieth century. Recent statistics show that nearly 70% of the Dominican population is urbanized (Krohn-Hansen 2016). Moya Pons (1998, 376–377) notes that Trujillo-era pro-natal policies encouraging childbearing were established to augment the Dominican workforce and simultaneously diminished the need for immigration policies in industries such as sugar. An increasingly mechanized industrialization of Dominican agricultural exports such as sugar, cacao, coffee, tobacco, and bananas exacerbated poverty in rural areas where small-scale farmers lost their lands to agribusinesses supported by government economic development policies to increase export crop production. All of these factors led to the rise of rural to urban migration to Dominican cities like Santo Domingo and "a new urban proletariat composed of the unemployed and day laborers, called *chiriperos*, who came to constitute a ready market for cheap labor in the urban economy" (Moya Pons 1998, 379). To accommodate these changes, new development policies in the 1950s included investment in building streets and parks, but there was no such expansion of food markets in new urban barrios (Murray 1996, 2). Therefore, new urban residents were distanced from public retail food venues, creating a new entrepreneurial niche in which corner stores closed this gap. While Derby's research shows the rise of colmados in rural areas as a response to deforestation to increase sugarcane production, Murray's important history establishes that today's preference for food shopping in colmados among the working poor and middle class began, essentially, as a popular response to restricted food access in dense urban areas.

While *El Colmado* provides us with an excellent snapshot of the significance of food shopping in colmados, there are limitations to using this text in the contemporary context since it was first published over twenty years ago and the island's demographics, economics, and politics have shifted during this time. First, while Murray's text provides extensive details on issues such as the role of shopkeepers and inventory purchasing, it provides only limited details on using in-store credit within colmados. Second, when Murray does discuss fiao, he notes that Haitians were summarily prohibited from fiao within colmados—a prohibition that did not exist in my own research. Third, there has been virtually no updated research on the recent distribution of colmados throughout the country nor on whether the aspiration to own and operate a colmado has changed. An exception to this is Krohn-Hansen's research (2013) on Dominican transnational migration and labor in New York focused on Dominican colmados in the United States, some of which are staffed by colmaderos who learned the trade as shopkeepers' assistants in the Dominican Republic before migrating to New York to work in a shop there. But for the last two decades, the role of colmados in the socioeconomic life of the Dominican Republic has been largely ignored, and exact figures as to how many people work as shopkeepers in the country is unknown. In fact, Carvajal (2017, 3) points out that

> Given the lower level of formality in this sector [the traditional food retail sector], there is almost no statistical information available on sales and operations [in the Dominican Republic]. Industry sources estimate that there are 50,000 colmados around the country and that they serve as a major source of informal

employment in both rural and urban areas. Though they are mainly individually-owned, there is at least one case in which a single person owns fifty colmados (similar to a franchising operation).

Carvajal (2017) also explains that there have been some substantial changes over time with regard to retail volume and range of services within colmados, but her report fails to indicate the timelines of these changes:

[Colmados] have increased their product and service offerings to accommodate a wider audience. Colmados have expanded, moving from offering an average of 300 products previously to over 1,500 products in their larger establishments. While focusing on the middle- and lower-income segments of the population, colmados provide a variety of additional services, which may include financing options, direct loans, and delivery services. In addition, many colmados function as bars and operate slot machines or other entertainment options.

Colmados in El Callejón and La Cienaga both substantiate and deviate from Carvajal's depiction. In fact, colmados in Cabarete provide some but not all of these services, and most colmados are not the "larger establishments" to which she refers, having implications for both shoppers and shopkeepers in these neighborhoods. In the next section, I describe the general look and feel of colmados in Cabarete and then compare and contrast colmados with supermarkets.

SUPERMARKETS AND COLMADOS COMPARED

At the time of my research, there were approximately thirty colmados[1] throughout Cabarete. It is thought that the etymology of the word *colmado* comes from the verb *colmar* which means to heap or to fill to the brim (Murray 1996; Krohn-Hansen 2013), a very fitting characterization for the ubiquitous small spaces that are packed not only with all kinds of goods but also provide different types of social and economic services for their customers. In other parts of the Caribbean, such as Cuba, Puerto Rico, and on the U.S. mainland, the word *bodega* is used instead of colmado, but with some differences. For example, in the neighborhood of Washington Heights in New York City, Dominican-run colmados are similarly small corner stores, like those in the Dominican Republic, but unlike their counterparts in the Caribbean, colmados in the United States are often open-shelved shops where shoppers can help themselves to the items they need (Regalado 2016). Dominican colmados, like those in El Callejón and La Cienaga, are usually closed-shelved shops, except for bulk vegetable and fruit bins that are typically placed near a corner store's entryway.

In Cabarete, there are some inherent differences between colmados and supermarkets of which all residents are astutely aware. The most basic difference between these two food shopping venues has to do with the shopping experience customers can expect in each. A store that allows shoppers to go up and down aisles to meet their own needs, regardless of the overall size of the store or volume of products it carries, is usually referred to as a *supermercado* in Spanish or even by the English word "supermarket." Cabarete has a total of two small independently owned supermarkets, Supermercado La Rosa and La Tienda. Based upon their small size and the low volume of products that are carried in each, La Rosa and La Tienda might be referred to as bodegas in other places, such as New York, Puerto Rico, or Cuba. In addition to these small grocers, Cabarete has one large, independently owned, big-box supermarket called Janet's. Shopping in big-box grocers is characterized by: products lying in full grasp of customers on open shelves; a greater volume and variety of products offered; in-house outlets offering services such as cell phone/internet and international money exchange; stores compartmentalized into distinct departments, such as meat, dairy, bakery, produce, liquor, and sundries; and a front-end consisting of many cashiers.

Unlike corner stores, which can be found within El Callejón and La Cienaga, all supermercados in Cabarete are located outside of working-class neighborhoods. Instead, these three supermarkets lie on the main highway: La Rosa lies just west of El Callejón, La Tienda is about 1 kilometer east of the Callejón, and Janet's is on the east side of Cabarete. The location of supermarkets makes them more amenable to area resorts and businesses catering to tourists and middle-income residents who, by and large, are Europeans or North Americans (from both Canada and the United States) working in local NGOs, schools, or businesses. In fact, the entrance to the neighborhood in Cabarete called ProCab, most known for housing expats, international tourists, and upper-class residents—what many residents of the Callejón and La Cienaga called *ricos*, or rich people—is right across the street from Janet's. There are no colmados in ProCab, which means the nearest grocer for people residing in ProCab is Janet's, strengthening the argument that Janet's is located to serve primarily that clientele.

In 2017, approximately 160 big-box grocery stores existed throughout the Dominican Republic, the majority of which reside in large urban areas, especially Santo Domingo, Santiago de los Caballeros, and San Francisco de Macorís (Carvajal 2017). These franchise grocery stores represent eight primary supermarket chains in the Dominican Republic: (1) Grupo Ramos, which owns La Sirena and Pola, two of the most well-known and most established big-box stores throughout the country, along with Aprezio Supermarkets; (2) Centro Cuesta Nacional, which owns Nacional, Jumbo, Jumbo Express, Cuesta Librería, and Cuesta Centro del Hogar supermarkets; (3) Plaza Lama; (4) Bemosa, with Bravo Supermarkets; (5) MercaTodo; (6)

PriceSmart, which is a Dominican American chain; (7) Carrefour; and (8) Olé Hypermarkets (Carvajal 2017). Of these eight chains, Carvajal's report (2017, 2) notes that "Grupo Ramos has the biggest reach and claims to be the largest employer and tax payer in the food retail sector."

In 2000, Janet's opened as a small, independent, family-run grocery store. Owned and operated by a Dominican couple, Janet and Gito, Janet's supermarket provides middle-class and international shoppers (both tourists and laborers in the tourism industry) a place to shop, particularly residents who reside in communities lying east and south of Sosúa. It is approximately 100 meters from the beach on the north side of State Road 5, conveniently situated where every bus, motoconcho, and other vehicle pass by. This supermarket is generally full of shoppers, from the time the doors open in the morning until they close in the evening. When compared to colmados and the smaller, bodega-like Supermercado La Rosa and La Tienda, Janet's is enormous. After a significant remodel that was completed in April 2015, Janet's is roughly 10,000 square feet.

In comparison to other food venues, Janet's sells a massive volume of products: from vegetables and fruit to sunglasses and beachwear. A great number of their processed food items are imported from all over the world, so that shopping up and down their aisles becomes a dizzying array of languages, packaging, and products. Janet's also provides a number of important services, such as providing in-house telecommunications outlets, Orange and Claro, two of the most prominent cell phone services in the country. It is in Janet's that most residents of Cabarete—expats, tourists, and working-class residents—come to renew their monthly cell plan, purchase a new cell phone, or put more minutes on their SIM card. Because the bulk of all cell phone users in town use Orange, I was quick to modify my interview questions with residents. I got a very different response from interviewees when I asked, "How often do you go to Janet's?" (to which they responded, at least once a month to buy minutes from Orange) and then when I asked, "How many times per week do you buy food at Janet's?" (responses were, without exception, "never" or "almost never"). Every interviewee expressed some version of Belkis' claim: "There is no way I could feed my kids and me if there weren't any corner stores around. [CH: How much of your food do you buy in a week at colmados?] All of it! [laughs] . . . Really, Cristina, I maybe buy a little something at Janet's not even once a month, and that's only when I go to Orange. [CH: When you do, what do you buy in Janet's?] [pauses, scrunches up her mouth, and rolls her eyes] Maybe an ice cream on a stick?"

But working-class residents of Cabarete, on the whole, do not shop in big-box stores because of the benefits they garner from shopping in colmados: much to the disappointment of global food supply chains (Mayol 2019). In 2007, the Dominican Republic signed the Central American-Dominican Republic Free

Trade Agreement (CAFTA-DR), an agreement the United States was hoping would augment U.S. imports, especially in the food industry, in the Dominican Republic and overall in the region. But colmados typically sell national and local products or international products produced through local franchises, such as Nestle in San Francisco de Macorís. Carvajal (2017) denotes that colmados are the primary venue of what is called the "traditional market channel" for food. The "modern retail channel" includes supermarket chains but also independent grocery stores like Janet's and convenience stores/gas stations (commonly referred to as *bombas* in Dominican Spanish). In fact, according to the most recent estimates, only 20%–25% of retail food sales are executed through supermarkets and 75%–80% of retail food purchases in the Dominican Republic are carried out in colmados (Mayol 2019), providing overwhelming evidence of the significance of colmados in the lives of the majority of shoppers.

Unlike shoppers' experiences in supermarkets, colmados' prices are fixed. There are no coupons, no sales, and no special offers in colmados. Everyone knows that the price of a product at one colmado will be the price at another. In both El Callejón and La Cienaga, residents report that they can't remember when a shopkeeper had a sale or undercut other colmados' prices. In fact, if they did so, people would be angry at them for trying to undercut other colmados and therefore their intention to attract more customers would backfire. Scholars have found similar results in other colmados throughout the country. For example, in Santiago de los Caballeros, the second largest city in the center of the Dominican Republic, Rosing (2007) found fixed prices in colmados, as did Murray (1996) in his ethnography of colmados in Santo Domingo a decade earlier. Shopping in colmados in Cabarete is predicated upon fair, predictable pricing that avoids price-gouging to attract more shoppers.

Yet, like Esther in the vignette at the beginning of this chapter, overwhelmingly shoppers exclaim that "everything is cheaper in [the supermarket]." And they're right: a price comparison of preferred items purchased by most families in the Callejón and La Cienaga revealed that in the supermarket, prices per unit where in fact less expensive. But supermarkets do not sell small quantities—for example, bags of homemade stewed beans or uncooked rice sold for 10 or 20 pesos. Instead, supermarket customers buy 15 ounce cans of unseasoned cooked beans or 5-pound bags of uncooked rice. These prepackaged supermarket products are sold in larger quantities, increasing the overall price, even while the price per unit is cheaper than what shoppers would pay in colmados. Gustavo, a fifty-four-year-old Dominican who moved to El Callejón from Baní in 2004, told me that

> You can buy bigger quantities of stuff at the supermarket, instead of buying your rice, your stewed beans daily for higher prices at the colmados. People buy

at colmados because they don't have the large sum of money to buy the large quantities of stuff found at the supermarket. [CH: Such as?] For example, they don't sell bulk rice at the supermarket, so you can't buy 15 pesos of rice for the day, you have to buy 150 pesos for the pre-packaged rice. This prohibits people from shopping [at the supermarket].

Gustavo made an important and astute observation: if residents did indeed buy prepackaged products at the big-box grocer, it would be cheaper by the unit, but they are unable to garner enough money to do so. Residents of El Callejón and La Cienaga often engage in piecemeal work in the tourist economy, such as motorcycle taxi drivers or vendors who sell trinkets to tourists at the beaches. People who engage in this type of work might earn between 100 and 1000 pesos a day, depending on the season. They don't earn a salary, only taking home what they make in a day after paying for their products (for vendors) and gas (either directly, for the taxi drivers, or indirectly, for the vendors getting from home to the beach). Therefore, buying large quantities of food at lower prices is not economically feasible, so colmados allow them to buy smaller quantities of food that cost more per unit (bag, pound, kilo, liter, etc.) than the prepackaged goods at the chain grocer.

Additionally, buying food on a daily basis cuts down on the need for cold storage. Buying a dozen eggs or a gallon of milk will need to be refrigerated, if not consumed within a certain amount of time. But in El Callejón and La Cienaga, there are scheduled and unscheduled blackouts. From 5:00 p.m. to 11:00 p.m. each day, there is no electricity in these neighborhoods unless people have bought a generator for their home. Often, there are also sporadic cuts to electrical services at other times of the day. Without reliable cold storage, large quantities of food and leftovers quickly spoil in this tropical environment. People shop daily in order to live within their economic means, but also to curb food waste due to electrical shortages.

But above all, interviewees indicate their preference for shopping at colmados when they are low on cash is because colmaderos allow certain shoppers to buy food and supplies on credit. Although buying food on credit is vital to provisioning their households, not all shoppers are afforded this privilege, something that is explained in more detail in chapter 3.

PROVISIONING HOUSEHOLDS: COLMADOS AND LO CRIOLLO

Residents of El Callejón and La Cienaga shop in colmados to some degree because it is precisely where they buy food considered lo criollo, the phrase Derby (1998) uses to refer to "homegrown" food. Residents in Cabarete refer to homegrown food as *comida criolla* in Spanish and *manje* (literally, "food") in Kreyòl. For all working-class residents, colmados are known as the place where lo criollo is established and renegotiated, depending on who is shopping, for whom they are cooking, and what they want to prepare. In fact, most Dominicans report that colmados are the place where they purchase preferred, recognizable products—products that they might or might not find if they shopped in Janet's, and if so, it would only be after wading through the vast amount of imported, foreign products lining Janet's shelves. For Haitians, they complain that no area food venue carries Haitian products, so they strive to find suitable substitutes that simulate desired tastes. Sometimes, Haitian residents note that while they might notice the differences in flavors when they use replacement ingredients, often their families do not, especially their children who were born in the Dominican Republic or those who migrated when they were very young.

Recognizing and identifying lo criollo is often contrasted with that which it is not. For example, Derby (1998) juxtaposes lo criollo with *lo extranjero* (literally, "the foreign"), which is something to be feared and shunned, in a well-known article detailing the development and effects of a rumor that circulated in 1992 when residents of Santo Domingo charged foreign-owned (*gringo*) high-yield chicken factories and fast-food chains like Pica Pollo with producing chicken "with worms." In the face of ever-increasing transnational trade between the Dominican Republic and the United States, Derby (1998, 479) writes that lo criollo came to hold an important place in the Dominican social imaginary:

> There is something deeply scandalous about gringo chickens. They are animals produced like machines. They are born to die, in enormous coops, and are never allowed to roam. Gringo chickens by homology also represent how Dominicans see life in the United States—confined in high-rises and trapped by the tentacles of the state. By contrast, the patio chicken represents the family because it is grown in the public extension of the house. It is typically Dominican because it is allowed free range . . . . The gringo chicken is cheaper and more beautiful (pure white, as opposed to the motley piebald—i.e., mulatto—Dominican bird), but lacks nourishment. It fills you up, but in an empty way. Most importantly, the gringo chicken, plain and simple, lacks *sabor*, or taste.

Numerous products sold in colmados are indeed some version of local foodstuffs, especially produce grown somewhere in the Dominican Republic; meat from animals kept in neighborhood pens or on nearby farms; and cheese, yogurt, and milk sold in vacuum-sealed boxes and small single-serving bags from dairies in Sosúa (see Wells (2009) for a thorough history of the dairy industry in Sosúa built by Jewish immigrants from Europe during World War

II). In one case, I found a colmado in La Cienaga that sold goat meat (*chivo* in Spanish, *cabrit* in Kreyòl) butchered to order. Goat meat is not a common product provided in colmados in Cabarete; instead, shoppers usually purchase goat in *carnicerías* (local butcher shops) to prepare popular dishes such as *chivo guisado* (Dominican goat stew) or *cabrit sos kreyòl* (a Haitian dish of goat in creole sauce). But a local family in La Cienaga has a goat herd, so one of the shopkeepers will butcher a goat when the family wants to cull the herd or if a customer makes a special order for goat. Colmados also carry industrial foods produced by international companies that are manufactured domestically; for example, Carnation evaporated milk and sweetened condensed milk cans, owned by Swiss-based Nestle, are manufactured in either Santo Domingo or San Francisco de Macorís, the third largest city in the Dominican Republic and only 83.2 kilometers away from Cabarete over the Cordillera Septentrional. Carnation canned milks are staples of both Dominican and Haitian cuisine, particularly for their central role in desserts, such as *arroz con leche* (rice pudding), and for beverages, such as *morir soñando* ("to die dreaming," in English, a blended drink of evaporated milk and orange juice), hot chocolate, and *café con leche* (coffee with milk).

Colmados are linked to lo criollo because they are shopping venues that carry recognized brands and foods that Dominicans and Haitians rely on to make homegrown food. Felicidad, a twenty-seven-year-old mother of two-year-old Marisol and four-year-old Kenya who lives in La Cienaga, exclaims that when it comes to buying homegrown food of all sorts, colmados are the place for residents to shop. "I have a brother who works [in a factory that cans] Carnation in San Francisco de Macorís. I show my kids the [Carnation] label and tell them their tío works there. I buy Carnation from Reynaldo's colmado at the top of the street. [CH: Can't you buy Carnation at Janet's, too?] Sure, but I don't . . . I shop at colmados. That's where I buy homegrown food."

"You can buy homegrown food at Janet's, too, Cristina. But I have to search for them in a sea of all kinds of other stuff," says Lovely, a twenty-one-year-old who migrated to the Callejón in 2010 from Fond Verette, in southern Haiti. Unlike colmados, supermarkets carry a wide variety of products, whose shelves are lined with not only up to six different brands of canned milks, but also products that are not used in creole cuisine, such as imported boxes of breakfast cereals, loaves of bagged white bread, bottles of wine, and snacks like granola bars or Pop Tarts. When I asked Lovely to tell me how often she frequents colmados and supermarkets and what she buys in each, she reported that she does almost all of her shopping in two colmados in the Callejón. Once a month, she buys more minutes for her cell phone at Janet's, and only then will she sometimes go down the aisles to find something she needs. But that is the only way she shops at Janet's: shopping for something specific, a brand she recognizes and uses in her cooking, as well as something she knows she can afford. "I never buy rice in Janet's because I have to buy big bags there," Lovely said, a common phrase I heard uttered by most residents in the Callejón and La Cienaga.

However, some residents of Haitian heritage indicate that they have to learn how to translate certain tastes from the selections of foods they find in Cabarete, and they lament the fact that they cannot find certain foods that they desire to make typical manje. Residents of Haitian heritage often indicated to me, as Lovely did, that despite the supermarket's wide range of product diversity from all over the world, "there are no Haitian products in Janet's . . . none at all. I can't find *petit mil* (dried millet), or . . . well, anything." Anouz, from Ouanaminthe in northern Haiti, just over the border from Dajabón, Dominican Republic, states, "Even though I make do with what I buy in colmados, I still can't find certain items, like djon-djon [a variety of black mushroom to make a typical northern Haitian dish, *diri ak djon-djon*, or rice with black mushroom]." She states that no food venues in Cabarete—not colmados, nor Janet's, nor any itinerant food sellers—carry items like black mushrooms. When I probed to see if she still made dishes like rice with black mushrooms by substituting with local ingredients, Anouz shared,

> Sometimes . . . but it has a different flavor. I don't make diri ak djon-djon, but I make other things with other ingredients I find here . . . My sos pwa [bean sauce] doesn't exactly taste like my mother's back home, but it's pretty close. And my sons don't know the difference. In fact, they were born here (Cabarete), so they think that what I make here is normal!

In one case, a local shopkeeper travels to purchase unattainable Haitian foods for herself and others in the neighborhood. Ana is a thirty-seven-year-old colmadera who travels back to her hometown in Haiti once every two months. Her mother and two aging sisters still live there, so she travels to look after them and bring them some food and money to help with household expenses. As she prepares to return to the Callejón, she fills her travel bags— bags that on her way to Haiti had been filled with Dominican products like big bags of rice and dried beans—with recognizable foods that Haitians living in the Callejón and La Cienaga have paid her a small fee to bring back with her, such as dried millet, sorghum, homegrown coffee from her aunt's farm, and raw sugar. According to all interviewees—both customers and shopkeepers alike—no other shopkeeper in Cabarete reported to provide this service. When I inquired as to how she crosses the border with goods in tow, Ana replied: "Well, I either cross at night on foot, avoiding the guard, or I give the guards a small tip so that they don't charge me." Ana was keenly aware that what she was doing was part of the extensive illicit trade that occurs at the border (Center for Strategic and International Studies 2019), although she scoffed about her role in this: "Because I bring so little back and forth that they [the guards] barely notice what I'm doing."[2]

Colmados are identified as lo criollo because of other benefits they provide. Since the Callejón and La Cienaga are home to working poor residents, there are very few adults at home each morning to prepare the typical time-intensive midday meal for families who take a break from their workdays to return home to eat. Colmados have become the primary venue where working women buy prepared foods in small bags to serve *la bandera*: the typical lunch consisting of stewed pinto beans, rice, and chicken called "the flag" because it consists of three parts and the Dominican flag is made up of three colors: red, white, and blue.

Marisa, a thirty-four-year-old Dominican born in Monte Cristi who moved to the Callejón in 2014, works as a maid in a well-known hotel on the beach, and during the high season, she works a daily shift from 6:00 a.m. to 1:30 p.m. or from 12:30 p.m. to 7:00 p.m. She is the mother of four children, all under the age of twelve. Her oldest, Wilcrys, an aspiring baseball player who trains at the Cabarete baseball academy every afternoon, attends seventh grade in a neighborhood private school during the morning school shift from 8:00 a.m. to 12:30 p.m. Her youngest three children, Deuris (nine years old), Demaris (eight), and Deywin (five), attend the afternoon school shift from 1:00 p.m. to 5:20 p.m. Marisa takes a motoconcho each day from her job and goes straight to Ana's colmado on 6th Street to buy prepared beans from doña Aleja, Ana's fifty-six-year-old sister-in-law who sets up a pot of beans just outside the colmado entrance and spoons beans into small, medium, and large bags for customers. Marisa then enters the colmado to purchase a 50 peso bag of uncooked rice and some chicken, usually a couple of wings, a leg, and a small breast to feed herself, her four children, and often her sister's husband, who lives across the street from them after having migrated to Cabarete eighteen months ago, leaving behind his wife and two children in Santo Domingo. "It's impossible for me to make the mid-day meal before I leave when my shift starts at 6am," says Marisa.

> Only when I start work at 12:30 can I make the mid-day meal in the morning. But buying prepared beans at Ana's colmado is so helpful—preparing the chicken and rice takes no time. It's the beans that need to be cooked right, all morning long, that's what we do with creole food. I can't send my kids to school, or have them come from school, and feed them a snack! They need real food, homegrown food, and the only way I can do this is by buying already cooked beans and then quickly getting the rice and chicken ready. [CH: So how important are colmados to you?] [Laughs] I can't do it without them!

Marisa's comments demonstrate the importance of eating lo criollo and the role colmados play in provisioning busy households with homegrown food, especially at midday. Her words also highlight the role women have as provisioners of households with homegrown food. While women do indeed play a primary role in provisioning households, they are not the only shoppers in colmados. As explained in the next section, women orchestrate household food shopping, but they are not always physically present as shoppers in colmados.

EVERYDAY LIFE IN COLMADOS

Colmado Behavioral Norms

In large measure, the hustle and bustle of neighborhoods like the Callejón and La Cienaga fluctuate according to the needs of people shopping in colmados. Most shopkeepers open their stores between 6:00 a.m. and 7:30 a.m. Each morning, residents can hear the tell-tale sounds of padlocks unlocking on nearby colmados' metal scroll doors followed by the screech of a door being lifted, signaling the start of a new day. At this early hour, usually the only shoppers trickling in are students buying candies or small buns for breakfast on their way to school. But by 8:00 a.m., traffic in colmados starts to pick up, when most women come shopping to buy ingredients they need to cook the midday meal. From 8:00 a.m. until about 11:15 a.m., 58% of the customers in colmados are women who enter the colmado announcing their presence with a nod to the shopkeeper or by saying "good morning." Most women buy five to eight items per visit, and most of these items are consumed that day. The most commonly purchased items in colmados during these hours are uncooked rice, uncooked beans, bouillon cubes (*sopita* or referred to by the brand name, Maggi) or liquid seasoning (*sazón*), cabbage, carrots, spices (such as cilantro or parsley), prepared stewed beans, and chicken (if the colmado sells freshly butchered or frozen meat).

There are certain behavioral norms in area colmados; most shoppers adhere to these norms without thinking and are keenly aware of them only when these norms are violated. In all colmados, throughout both the Callejón and La Cienaga, Spanish was the language used most often in transactions, regardless of who owned the shop or the ethnic backgrounds of the shoppers and shopkeepers. Colmaderos of Haitian heritage only spoke in Kreyòl to customers who addressed them in Kreyòl; at my count, only three out of every ten interactions used Kreyòl in colmados owned by shopkeepers of Haitian heritage. Overall, most shopkeepers start their encounter with a short "*dime* (tell me)," and the shopper responds with "*dame* . . . (give me . . .)," followed by the items they need. Yet if the shopkeeper knows the customer, this typical greeting may vary. I have heard both male and female shopkeepers modify their greeting by calling shoppers: (1) some form of kin term, such as *abuela* (grandmother), *tía* (aunt), or *hermana* (sister), even when none of the shoppers addressed as such was related to the shopkeeper; (2) a term of endearment, such as my *mi amor* (my love), *corazón* (sweetheart), or *amiga* (friend); (3) some sort of racial term, more often than not *morena* (for a person who was known to speak Kreyòl or who has very dark skin), and (4) a common word pointing up physical characteristics, such as *gordita* (little fat woman), *flaca* (skinny woman), or *rubia* (blondie; this word also refers to a person with very light skin). Although less frequently, I heard three shopkeepers use the word *gringa* (foreigner) to refer to customers who they thought might be tourists or part-time residents.

Customers do not queue up to be served. To keep order, colmaderos need to keep a keen eye out for when customers enter their shop, and amazingly, I found most shopkeepers had an uncanny sense of when to call on which shopper in the order they arrived. Colloquial forms of addressing customers are used as a way to help shopkeepers distinguish to whom they are speaking—an important function, since out of necessity, shopkeepers need to keep order and not offend customers. But these forms of address also help create and recreate bonds between shopkeeper and shoppers. Calling shoppers kin terms, such as grandmother or aunt, is reserved for women who are older than the shopkeeper, especially those shoppers who frequent that particular colmado and/or buy food on credit, which I explain in chapter 3. For those shoppers who are not allowed to buy food on credit, or who are less well known by the shopkeeper, the forms of address used are more likely to be a term of endearment, like my love or sweetheart; a racial term, such as morena or rubia; or a term highlighting physical characteristics, such as gordo or flaca. Those shoppers with whom the shopkeeper is not familiar are often those who are addressed without any form of address, only the standard, *Dime* (tell me).

Sometimes, shoppers enter a crowded colmado and hope to be served before others who have been waiting their turn. She might try to catch the shopkeeper's eye and say "dame" before the shopkeeper acknowledges her. When this occurs, other shoppers very infrequently express their dismay, sometimes with an eye roll or an exclamation charging favoritism just loud enough for the shopkeeper to overhear. Jherileidy, for example, tried to catch Edison's eye one morning, announcing to shoppers that her work as a launderer in a nearby hotel had kept her later than usual, postponing the start of cooking her midday meal. There were nine women waiting to be served when Jherileidy entered the colmado. The shopkeeper ignored her at first, nodding to the next customer in line. But Jherileidy, appealing to both the next shopper and Edison, said that she needed to finish cooking so that she could attend a parent-teacher meeting that started at 1:30 p.m.—the beginning of the school day for students who were enrolled in the afternoon session of one of the neighborhood's elementary schools. Two other customers ahead of her in line told her that they, too, had to attend the same meeting, to which Jherileidy replied that they have fewer mouths to feed than she does, apparently meaning that she would need more time to prepare more food for her family than the other customers. Edison seamlessly looked over to Jherileidy and acknowledged her with an almost whispered "*bueno* (ok)," and without his characteristic smile. The woman next in line rolled her eyes and looked to other customers for solidarity, as she indicated to Jherileidy with her scrunched up lips and a shake of her head while the other women in line tsk-tsked but remained silent.

Demographic Shopping Patterns

While almost 60% of morning customers are women, about 37% of customers who shop throughout the morning are children of all ages. Typically, children shop in colmados for two reasons: (1) they enter colmados on their way to school, usually before 8:00 a.m., to purchase a breakfast-on-the-go of a small empanada, cornmeal bun (*arepa*), or small candies as treats, and (2) they are sent to the store by family members, usually grandmothers, aunts, or mothers, to buy last-minute items needed for the midday meal, such as a single-serving sack of seasoning for stewed beans or Carnation canned milk for coffee or hot chocolate. Wilson, a charming ten-year-old, comes to Gregorio's colmado in La Cienaga a few mornings a week. He lives with his mother and his four siblings. Wilson is the second oldest and is a fifth grader in the afternoon session at a private school, where he earned a scholarship because of his good grades. The rest of his siblings attend school in the mornings at the neighborhood public school. Wilson's twenty-eight-year-old mother, Wilma, launders clothes in her home and is paid by the piece. Between laundering clothes and preparing the midday meal, Wilma is tied to her home for most of the morning and finds it helpful that she can trust Wilson to shop for her when she needs it. When I asked Wilson about shopping in colmados, he told me,

> Gregorio knows me well, so when I enter the colmado he doesn't ignore me like other shopkeepers can sometimes do. [CH: Do you wait in line with the other shoppers to be served?] Yes, I wait in line, but often Gregorio nods at me, lets me know he sees me, and sometimes I whisper and he gets me what I need at the same time he is helping someone else. [CH: Do you pay with cash?] Sometimes I pay with cash, but mostly Gregorio writes down what I owe in the notebook. My mother trusts him to write in the real amount, I don't even stay to make sure that he writes down the right amount.

After the morning hours, the pattern of shoppers in area colmados changes. Instead of mostly women and children, afternoon and evening customers are typically split among women (30%), men (50%), and children/adolescents (20%). After the midday meal, shoppers tend to buy only one or two items, the most common of which are single-serving bags of powdered soap for washing machines (household laundry is sometimes attended to after the midday meal by an older daughter or mothers, once their work outside of the home or the school day is completed), salami sticks (commonly cut up in coins and fried for a light dinner or breakfast the next morning), eggs, small candies (purchased by children), 5-gallon jugs of potable water, bags of ice, and beer/liquor. Typically, men frequent colmados on their way home from work, from 5:00 p.m. till the colmado closes. Men are sometimes sent to colmados by their spouses or other family members, just as children are in the mornings by their mothers. When they are sent, men purchase whatever they are told to purchase; in this sense, patterns of shopping in colmados is similar to the patterns revealed in Marjorie DeVault's now classic work on the different ways in which men and women in heterosexual couples shop in the early 1990s in the United States (1991): both men and women shop, but it is women who labor to organize and orchestrate the provisioning of their household needs.

Foot traffic in area colmados lessens in the heat of the afternoons, making this a great time to interview colmaderos. Josué, a forty-eight-year-old Haitian shopkeeper in the Callejón, describes everyday dynamics in colmados as the afternoon wanes, detailing the transition from colmado to colmadón each evening for the handful of colmados that do so in these working-class neighborhoods:

> I start to see more and more men come to my shop [CH: Starting around what time?] . . . oh maybe around 5, they come because their women [spouses] send them for something, usually to take care of replacing their [5-gallon] water jug. Men sometimes carry it back to their houses or spend a few pesos and send it home on the back of a motoconcho. When they do that, men stay at the colmado, buy a cold beer, maybe a bottle of rum or beer and disposable cups to share with others, play dominos, turn on the radio, and the colmado gets crowded again— not because of shoppers, like women who come in the morning, but guys who stay and drink and talk to friends [CH: Sort of like a bar?] Well, yeah, a little like a bar, but I don't have darts and billiards, or even a proper dance floor.

Colmados as gendered spaces fluctuate throughout the day: as shoppers, there are women and kids in the mornings and a mix of people in the early afternoons, and to complete short orders for their households and to socialize, evenings in colmados consist primarily of men. Many women and girls told me throughout my fieldwork that no one expects them to shop in colmados toward the end of the day. Neila, a sixteen-year-old Dominican girl who is completing her high school equivalency certificate in the area night school, echoes the sentiments of many of my interviewees when she said: "My mom sends me to the colmados quite often throughout the week, but I wouldn't go to a colmado at night [she gestures with her hands, mimicking a bottle being tipped back to her mouth]. [CH: You don't feel comfortable there at that time?] No way, friend, that's not my time to be there." When I asked her if she had had any uncomfortable or dangerous encounters at a colmado/colmadón at night, she shook her head slowly and replied, "No, not really, but there's always the comment made, you know, about my clothes, my hair . . . I just don't like it."

"KEEP[ING] OUR BELLIES FULL": LABORING IN AND THROUGH COLMADOS

Another important facet of colmados as a total social phenomenon in the Callejón and La Cienaga is their capacity as sites of labor flows or bringing people together who learn to labor within networks of colmados. Colmados are not only sites of consumption, but they are also sites of production and distribution. Shopkeepers are not the only people who work in colmados. Colmaderos orchestrate the flow of labor through colmados that literally keeps their neighbors in business. Many residents told me that without colmados, "we wouldn't keep our bellies full," says Yaritza, "not just because I buy my food there, but because so many people work through colmados." Shopkeepers hire all kinds of people to fill other important roles that serve their customers: those who work within colmados, such as the young men who act as front-end managers called *ayudantes* (assistants), and others with whom shopkeepers informally contract to provide services, such as moto-conchistas, motorcycle taxi drivers who make deliveries from colmados to people's homes. Taking shopkeepers, ayudantes, and motoconchistas in turn, I show that by varying degrees, each role is mediated by salient constructions of gender and kinship.

In both Murray's (1996) and Krohn-Hansen's (2016) research on col-maderos in other places, colmados are owned by men. Corroborating this research, colmaderos in Cabarete also are often men. But a surprising finding was that out of about thirty colmados in the Callejón and La Cienaga, five of them were owned or partly owned and operated by women: two women in La Cienaga (Bella and Rosalín) and three in El Callejón (Anouz, Ana, and Micayla). Four out of these five women co-own the colmado, like Micayla and her husband, Junior, who co-own the eponymous Colmado Junior. Ana, the Haitian colmadera who travels to Haiti periodically and returns with Haitian products for area residents, was the only woman who fully owned her own colmado, and her colmado is named after her. Besides Ana's, there is only one other colmado in Cabarete with a woman's name on the sign. Colmado Inés is named after the colmadero's wife, but she does not own and rarely works in the colmado. That's her husband's domain.

Shopkeepers who worked in the twelve colmados in which I conducted participant -observation were thirty-seven to sixty-eight years old. The ethnic background of all shopkeepers in the region varied as well. Twenty-one colmados in the Callejón and La Cienaga are run by Dominicans, with another eight colmados operated by Haitians and one owned by a Dominican of Haitian heritage, a thirty-four-year-old man named Jonás. His mother, of Haitian descent who grew up in a nearby Dominican community called Batey Libertad, migrated to Cabarete with her three children in 2001, when Jonás was nineteen. He was an ayudante in a colmado in La Cienaga for five years before he moved to Dajabón to work with his godfather in the market there, mostly selling produce from their family's small farm and "anything else we could get our hands on."

Most colmaderos hire ayudantes through their networks of kin. For example, Yeriel, Yaritza's nineteen-year-old long-term boyfriend, is an ayudante in Edison's colmado in the Callejón. Yeriel is Edison's oldest brother's third child. He is the second boy from this family to work with Edison as an ayudante. Oliver, Yeriel's older brother and the oldest child out of six, used to work with Edison until he moved to Santiago to work in his mother's brother's colmado in the city, "almost downtown," Yeriel exclaims when I ask him the location of his maternal uncle's colmado. Because it is located in a desirable location, Yeriel's uncle's colmado in Santiago is more economically solvent than Edison's and has a lot more inventory. His uncle needed an ayudante who had experience with lots of distributors and could keep pace with the heavy foot traffic typically seen in Edison's colmado in the Callejón, one of the busiest and most lucrative colmados in Cabarete. Yeriel's expectation is that, like his brother, his work in Edison's colmado is seen as one step on the path to working in a bigger corner store someday for one of his relatives in the Dominican Republic. Because of this upwardly mobile trajectory, commonly ayudantes start their positions at sixteen years old and age out of this job by about twenty-four years old, when it is expected for them to move on to other jobs, maybe even work toward owning their own colmado or becoming a partner, or *socio* in Spanish (a process Krohn-Hansen (2016) explains in detail in U.S. colmados).

A typical colmado ayudante serves multiple functions, something that Yeriel speaks about with pride: "Each day, I get people's orders from behind the counter and ring them up, and then I review the distributors' orders who come with their products each day. I need to make sure that they deliver what Edison orders." Sometimes, ayudantes work alongside colmaderos, particularly during the busy mornings when people shop for the midday meal. Ayudantes, in these cases, are sometimes adolescent girls, most likely a relative (daughters, granddaughters, or nieces) of shopkeepers. They do not work a daily work shift but might work every Tuesday or Thursday, like thirteen-year-old Romely does for her grandfather, Josué, in the Callejón. Romely's job is to mark down how much people owe in the in-store credit notebook once her grandfather has told after each order he completes. Other ayudantes who work alongside colmaderos, like Demaris, are put to work finding requested items behind the counter while the colmadero adds everything up and records shoppers' debts in the notebook. These positions are more short-lived than ayudantes who work alone in colmados—usually ending when the girl graduates from high school, moves into another role (such as becoming a mother), or gets another job doing something else.

Both Janet's and colmados make deliveries, but there are some differences between them. Janet's minivan delivers to people during the hours that it is opened for business. Janet's is open 8:00 a.m. to 8:00 p.m., Monday through Saturday, and 8:30 a.m. to 1:30 p.m. on Sundays. Colmados, on the other hand, typically open their doors between 6:00 a.m. and 7:30 a.m. and stay open until 9:00 p.m. or later, especially if they are transformed into colmadones in the evening—a place where people, often men, come to listen to music, drink beer or rum, play dominos or dance, and socialize. But beyond the hours of daily operation, colmados are commonly known for providing around the clock customer service. In fact, there's a saying that "colmaderos never sleep." Residents can call a colmadero after hours, request items, and pay for them to be delivered to their homes. Customers who request these delivery services are usually charged a flat fee, which in 2015 was 50 pesos a delivery, no matter how many items were delivered. But distance between colmado and the delivery destination was sometimes considered. For example, Justína, a fifty-three-year-old Dominican grandmother raising her youngest child's two children, aged ten and fourteen, lives in La Cienaga. She told me that

I usually call Bella if I need something delivered in the middle of the night. Anita [her youngest granddaughter] had a fever last week and we ran out of drinking water at midnight. So I called Bella who had a 5-gallon water jug delivered to my house. [CH: Bella's colmado is right around the corner from your house. Would you ever call Edison, whose colmado is in the Callejón?] No, I would pay too much or they would tell me to call a nearby colmado. [CH: How much more would you pay for that?] Actually, I think it would be more like 100 pesos, but I'm not really sure because no one does that.

   While Janet's provides delivery services via a delivery van, complete
with its logo on the side door, colmado deliveries are made motoconchistas
on motorcycles and scooters, which are especially useful to speed around
cars on all of the dirt roads throughout the Callejón and La Cienaga and on
the only paved thoroughfares through each neighborhood. Besides deliver-
ing colmado orders, motoconchistas are an essential mode of transportation
for everyone, since very few residents in these working poor neighborhoods
own any sort of personal vehicle, such as a family car or scooter. Nino, a
local motoconchista, moved to the Callejón in 2005 from Nagua, a bustling
city four hours east of Cabarete on State Road 5. He worked his way up
the local economic hierarchy to land the enviable position of parking his
motorcycle at the motorcycle taxi stop at the entrance of the Callejón with
other motoconchistas with seniority. Parking his motorcycle at this location, which was equidistant to the tourist zone and to local colmados, gave
him more visibility with shopkeepers and tourists who were shopping or
making their way to the beach.
   Most of Nino's clients are shopkeepers who hired him to make deliveries
to customers living throughout the Callejón. Making deliveries for colmados encompasses about 75% to 80% of his business. For a fee of 50 pesos
(approximately US$1.16), motoconchistas are hired when shopkeepers call
motoconchistas for customers who either call the colmado ahead of time with
an order or for those who come to colmados to shop and buy too much to
bring home by foot. As a more senior motoconchista in the Callejón, Nino's
earnings are a bit higher than other motorcycle taxi operators in the area.
Nino reports that on a typical day during the high tourist season (from June
to September, December to February, and the weeks between Carnaval and
Easter), he sometimes earns up to 2,000 pesos a day, but more characteristic weekly earnings approximate the same amount in a week, which hardly
covers his expenses. During my fieldwork, the cost of gas was, on average,
US$7.50 per gallon,[3] and Nino was required to pay monthly fees to the local
union of motoconchistas (4,500 pesos, approximately US$102). Some newer
motoconchistas also have a monthly payment for their motorcycle, something
that Nino finished paying two years prior, that could run them up to about
1,000 pesos a month, depending upon the quality of the vehicle. In order to
receive calls from shopkeepers, all motoconchistas need a reliable cell phone
and enough minutes on their account to make and receive calls—another
expense shouldered by motoconchistas. Despite the high costs of being a
professional motorcycle taxi driver, it is one of the most lucrative jobs in
the area, especially for men with no high school or post-secondary degree.
Colmados, then, are an important relational space (Harvey 2006; Low 2009)
through which people and money flow in these working-class neighborhoods;
as spaces they are sites of consumption (shopping) as well as production (job

creation and maintenance). In fact, without colmados, residents like Nino might never have migrated to Cabarete in the first place.

CONCLUSIONS

Colmados have been called a total social phenomenon in the Dominican Republic because of cultural, social, and economic reasons. The ubiquity of food shopping in colmados in the Dominican Republic developed over time due to both increased state investment in industrial agriculture as well as the rise of urbanization. By the mid-twentieth century, large-scale sugar plantations deforested lands once used for small-scale family farms and hunting grounds, forcing the rural population to migrate to urban centers in search of employment. While government spending for growing cities burgeoned during this period, there was less attention paid to expanding public markets to feed urban newcomers, leaving a gap that was filled by the rise of small, corner stores throughout the country. With dwindling prospects to farm and rising rural-urban migration, being a shopkeeper became a coveted position. Big-box chain supermarkets exist in the Dominican Republic, like Janet's in Cabarete, but shopping in colmados is preferred by most people, especially among residents of the Callejón and La Cienaga.

Colmados appeal to shoppers for a variety of reasons. Most customers are interested in buying small quantities of products in no small part because irregular electric outages lead to problems with food spoilage. Although supermarkets may provide products at a lower cost per unit, shopping in supermarkets is not practical because of the way goods are packaged and sold in larger quantities, which in the end cost more per shopping trip than goods sold in colmados. As part of the local foodscape in these working-class neighborhoods, colmados are spaces that carry recognizable homegrown foods for both Dominicans and Haitians to create lo criollo, including comida criolla and manje. While Haitians do lament the fact that area food venues—both colmados and supermarkets—fail to carry certain Haitian products, shopping at colmados allows them to produce manje well enough with flavors that they desire and recognize, depending on what types of food they are cooking and for whom.

There are few spaces in the Callejón and La Cienaga that are more economically and socially active, particularly with respect to building and fostering relationships, than colmados. Colmados bring people together and are key sites of relational space, not only for the sake of consumption, such as shopping, but also for production, as in the flow of workers who fill their bellies because of colmados, such as motoconchistas. Colmados also make and remake social bonds revolving around kinship and gender. Shopkeepers refer to some of their most loyal and frequent customers using kin terms, even when shoppers and shopkeeper are not related. Women are the primary provisioner of households, but they are not the only shoppers to frequent colmados. Because women direct men and children to colmados with lists of items in hand, shopkeepers assist all kinds of shoppers throughout the day. Some colmados transition into colmadones at the end of the day, where men stop in to shop but stay to socialize, listen to music, and relax with a drink. In these ways, colmados bring people together to reproduce and nurture the family, the community, and individuals.

But for the residents of La Cienaga and the Callejón who work in the vulnerable tourism economy, even shopping each day in small quantities at a neighborhood colmado is financially difficult. To ease their burden, shopkeepers allow customers to make purchases on a tab, using in-store credit, which has become an institution throughout the country. The next chapter explains the rules and norms of fiao and the evolving moral discourses about fiao in Cabarete.

NOTES

1. Definitively counting colmados is challenging because colmados often are attended to intermittently, as colmaderos migrate to other places, and/or fall into financial ruin, a topic I take up in chapter 4.

2. Many Dominicans think that Ana's actions are typical of Haitians who live in the Dominican Republic, and that the Dominican Republic is suffering from untaxed Haitian goods entering the Dominican Republic. However, most of the illicit trade in goods at Haitian Dominican border crossings are products going from the Dominican Republic to Haiti. The pattern of cross-border trade is asymmetric; in 2017 the Center for Strategic and International Planning reported $853 million of Dominican exports went to Haiti, while just $42 million Haitian products were imported to the Dominican Republic. The same report showed that of the $853 million Dominican exports to Haiti, $634 million goes untaxed in Haiti; in other words, these are uncollected monies the Haitian government could use to improve social services and infrastructure. It is surmised that these goods are untaxed by Haiti because of mismanagement or corruption (i.e., Haitian guards being bribed to look the other way).

3. For the most part, the Dominican Republic uses the metric system, but gasoline is typically sold by the gallon.

Chapter 3

"Pa' la Dignidad"

Fiao and the Emergent Moralities of Being Responsible

October 3, 2014

Waiting for our dinner to cook over an open fire, Amelia, Luisa, Samuel, Daniel, and I were seated around a square plastic table in Pista Motocross, a small neighborhood of 50 homes about 5km east of Janet's supermarket down State Road 5. Every few minutes, Luisa or Amelia walked over to the 18-inch in diameter metal pot resting carefully on three cement blocks at the center of a wood-fire pit to stir the sancocho, a quintessential Caribbean stew made from a mix of meats and vegetables with plenty of savory spices. Earlier this morning, Luisa and I traveled up and down the Callejón—stopping at three colmados and a butcher shop—shopping for ingredients for the stew after she completed her job washing two families' clothes earlier that morning. Amelia, Luisa, and I had been preparing food, talking, listening to music, and taking care of Luisa' 2-year old grandson, Deywin, for over four hours when Samuel and Daniel joined us as we waited for the simmering sancocho.

Amelia moved to Cabarete in 2010 from La Vega, a small city south of Santiago in the center of the country well known for its raucous Carnival celebration. She works as an assistant manager in a local tourist shop, a coveted professional position that she has been hired for, in no small part, because she has completed a two-year program in tourism-focused business and speaks some English. Amelia and Luisa are neighbors who support each other in everything from sharing food to raising children; between them, they have cared for five children, two grandchildren, and a niece. Luisa, one of the few residents of Cabarete who was actually born in the Callejón, works in the informal economy as a caretaker of "rich" people's vacation homes through-out Cabarete and the nearby community of Sabaneta de Yásica. When these vacation homes are occupied during the tourist season, Luisa is hired to do daily housecleaning and cooking, and once a week washes laundry and does

83

some light gardening, mostly watering lawns. Daniel is a 35-year old Haitian man who speaks fluent French, ideal for communicating with snowbirds from Quebec who hire him as a gardener—cutting trees, mowing lawns, and cleaning the pool each day. Samuel and Daniel have only lived in Pista Motocross for a year. Daniel lives with Samuel and Samuel's wife Aurelys, renting a small two-bedroom cottage up the street from Amelia and Luisa. Samuel, of Haitian heritage and originally from Santo Domingo, is currently out of work but a carpenter by trade; he and Daniel met when Samuel was hired for a construction job on a house in Cabarete where Daniel worked as a gardener.

I had only met Samuel and Daniel that morning, but I have known Luisa and Amelia for the better part of a year; Luisa and I met one day at the Cabarete ball park (the park well-known affectionately as, "El Play") while our children were at baseball practice, and including today, my children and I have eaten with Amelia, Luisa, and their families about a dozen times. The conversation around the table was light-hearted and easy-going, spoken in a much slower Spanish than is typical for Dominicans; I found that in Cabarete, when group conversations included Dominicans and Haitians, one of two things occurred: either the entire conversation slowed down, or Haitians stayed silent or near silent. Amelia told Samuel and Daniel that I'm a professor from North America learning more about life in Cabarete, especially about shopping in colmados and buying food using in-store credit.

At hearing my interest in colmados and fiao, both men started talking at once. Samuel told us that he mainly shops at Colmado Junior in the Callejón, where he has an open line of in-store credit. He likes that Junior, the colmadero, works there each day so he doesn't have to talk to his ayudante, Josef, with whom Samuel doesn't like to interact because Josef is known for his abrasive style of reminding customers about how much they owe in front of other shoppers. "It's none of their business what I owe," said Samuel. "We all owe something, but they don't have to know how much." Over the last few weeks, Daniel has started to date Sintia, a woman who sells jewelry on the beach who lives with a friend in La Cienaga, and Daniel has started to spend some nights there each week. Sintia's home is next door to the colmado owned by Rosalín and Enrique, and last week, Sintia and Daniel shopped together in the colmado while Rosalín was working. Daniel was allowed in-store credit to make his purchases because he was with Sintia. "She told Rosalín to put what I spent under her name in the notebook," Daniel told us. He hopes that this is the start of having his own page in Rosalín's notebook. "With a little time, after Rosalín sees I pay my debts [to Sintia], they'll give me my own tab," he speculated, optimistically.

Amelia listened intently to Samuel and Daniel, looking at me all the while and saying, "See?" When Daniel and Samuel finished their stories, Amelia looked over to them and said, "She [scrunching up her lips and looking my way] wants to know if Haitians get in-store credit, and we've [meaning her-self and Luisa] told her that you do. Fiao, it's for dignity [pa' la dignidad]. Without it, we just don't eat . . . not only shoppers, but also colmaderos. They need us, too," to which Luisa nodded her head and said, *"sí."*

Like Amelia, Luisa, Samuel, and Daniel, most working-class people who live and work in Cabarete shop using in-store credit in colmados. As indicated in chapter 2, the ability to use fiao in corner stores was the key factor for why residents shop in area colmados and refrain from shopping in the big-box store, Janet's. More often than not, customers shop in colmados without money. Fiao is ubiquitous in the Dominican Republic; it is, without a doubt, a lifeline for most residents, the only way that people can purchase food until they get paid. Adding to this, borrowers are allowed to pay down their debt as they are able to; in interview after interview with shopkeepers, they reported that it is infrequent that borrowers pay their debts in full, rather repaying a part of the debt while simultaneously purchasing more items and incurring more debt. For residents in the Callejón and La Cienaga, daily life is signified by the normal phenomenon of being in a perpetual state of indebtedness. Provisioning their households, their very survival, is dependent upon from whom they can borrow and how much debt they are allowed to incur.

Fiao is not only used within colmados but is found in other establishments as well. But this doesn't mean that everyone is afforded in-store credit in every venue nor does it mean that an open line of in-store credit remains available forever. While indebtedness is normal, there are norms for where, how, and if people are allowed in-store credit. Fiao is a social contract between shoppers and colmaderos in a system of balanced reciprocal exchanges. Determining a customer's eligibility for in-store credit is a complicated process, not to be taken lightly: shopkeepers must quickly evaluate customers for their ability to pay off their loan in a timely manner so that both colmaderos and shoppers mutually benefit from the exchange.

This chapter discusses the logistics of fiao in the Dominican context, paying special attention to how fiao is invoked for whom and how the process of using credit unfolds in colmados. This paves the way for a better understanding of how fiao in the Dominican Republic is similar to and different from in-store credit in other corner stores, in other places, in other times. In the Callejón and La Cienaga, there are three types of fiao given in colmados, and there are moral values and judgments that intersect with people's perceptions of these different types of debt. Even when indebtedness is perceived to be normal, in interactions involving fiao, it is sometimes denounced and vilified. In other words, fiao is tied up with cultural conceptions of moral personhood and is articulated as good and bad, sometimes by the same person in the same breath. Fiao is imbued with meaning, especially between and among groups of people—shoppers and store owners, men and women, working-poor people, and middle-class aspirants—with varying degrees of power. Assorted conceptions of fiao have implications for what it means to be recognized as hardworking or not. While fiao helps to relieve the precarity of residents' lives in the Callejón and La Cienaga, fiao is not always favorably perceived nor does everyone appreciate it as a strategy to attain dignity. Dignity for some residents means borrowing responsibly; for others, it means not borrowing at all.

FIAO IN CABARETE'S COLMADOS

Peebles (2010, 227) defines credit as "a method of lending concrete resources to an institution or an individual in the present and demanding (or hoping for) a return in the future." In the Dominican Republic, fiao is a system of balanced reciprocal exchanges in the form of lending credit and repaying debt between and among distributors, shopkeepers, and customers. Customers request fiao from shopkeepers by asking some version of "put it on my tab": *fíame?* or *dame fiao* in Spanish, and in Kreyòl, *kredit* or *ban m kredit?* Sometimes, customers just say, "cuaderno" (notebook). Shopkeepers always have their notebook on hand at the shop's counter for those customers who don't have money to cover their purchases, either in whole or in part. These notebooks look like the wire spiral-bound, white-lined ones that school children use in school.

When a shopper asks to buy food on credit, the shopkeeper makes a decision to allow the purchase or not, and if allowed, writes the borrowed sum in the notebook under the person's name. Sometimes, the person has a long column of debt in the notebook; sometimes there are sums that are scratched out and rewritten, indicating that some of their debt had been repaid. Debts are typically paid every fifteen days, called a *quincenal*, when workers are paid in the Dominican Republic. If borrowers cannot pay the whole debt, then it is expected that they will pay part of it. Shoppers know how much they owe each colmado because shopkeepers record the amount of the debt on a piece of a cardboard box and distribute it to each shopper so they keep track of their tab as the end of the quincenal nears.

Chapter 2 contends that colmados are a total social phenomenon in the Dominican Republic, and fiao is indeed an important part of the colmado experience. But fiao is not an equal opportunity phenomenon, as it is irregularly available and everyone must learn where, when, if, and how it is offered as they engage in daily life. In the Callejón or La Cienaga, I never encountered a colmado that categorically failed to offer in-store credit to customers the shopkeeper deemed capable of paying off their debt, known as gente responsable. This is unlike Murray's (1996) findings in which, in the

Figure 3.1   The Fiao Notebook. Photo taken by the author.

mid-1990s in colmados in Santo Domingo, he found some colmaderos had hung signs in their corner stores indicating that they would not lend in-store credit to anyone. Also, both Murray (1996) and Rosing (2009) found that colmados in Santo Domingo and Santiago, respectively, would categorically fail to offer in-store credit to Haitians. This was not so in Cabarete, and I explain this in detail in chapter 4.

Yet there was one category of shopper that was systematically ineligible for fiao: it was common knowledge in Cabarete that a tourist, especially an international tourist, would always be turned down if they asked for in-store credit. Elías, a forty-eight-year-old shopkeeper in La Cienaga, explains why he unconditionally denies fiao to tourists: "I never give fiao to tourists . . . well, usually they don't ask for it. But when they do, which happens from time to time, I tell them no. They're going to leave, I can count on them leaving, so I can't count on them paying their bill before they leave [Cabarete]." Figure 3.2 is the only example of a sign I found in Cabarete that prohibits fiao. It is not a coincidence that this sign is written in English, considered the lingua franca of tourists to the region, signifying the message's audience is international tourists; in Cabarete colmados, I never found a sign written in Spanish or Kreyòl with a message prohibiting fiao like this one.

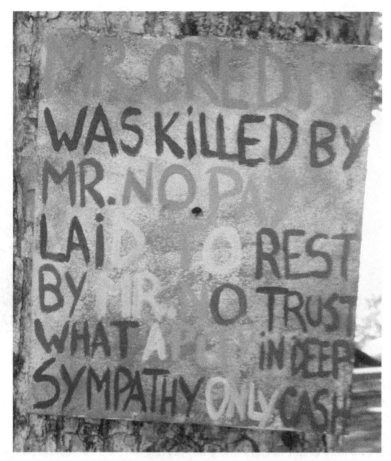

Figure 3.2   Sign Prohibiting Fiao in English. Photo taken by the author.

While fiao is ubiquitous in colmados, it is not guaranteed in other retail establishments, illustrated at the state-run public venue that sells lottery tickets in figure 3.3 in which "no one will be given fiao" is written in Spanish, ensuring that local residents understand and avoid requesting it. Fiao is also offered in other venues, such as the furniture shop depicted in figure 3.4, indicating "Todo Fiao" (Everything Fiao); this means that fiao may be available to customers who are deemed worthy by shopkeepers.

This furniture shop is located in Sosúa, not Cabarete, the significance of which is not lost on working-class residents of the Callejón and La Cienaga. When I showed Isaiys the photo of this furniture shop, he retorted: "I have never shopped there . . . I don't know anyone that has. Yes, it says todo fiao, but they don't mean it . . . not everyone can use in-store credit there. [CH: Who can, do you think?] (Shrugs his shoulders) I don't know . . . rich people."

Figure 3.3   Sign Prohibiting Fiao in Spanish. Photo taken by the author.

In the same way that not everyone is eligible for fiao in the furniture store in Sosúa, not everyone is eligible for in-store credit in colmados in La Cienaga and El Callejón. Those people who pay down their debt, even parts of their debt, in a timely manner are considered gente responsable. Being gente responsable is essential to getting a page in a shop's cuaderno, meaning that they are eligible to buy food with in-store credit. But if the customer fails to pay their debts at any time, the colmadero reserves the right to deny in-store credit to that customer. Additionally, being eligible for in-store credit at one colmado does not authorize a customer's eligibility for fiao in another colmado. In the Callejón and La Cienaga, at any one time, a typical customer might be deemed eligible for fiao in one or two colmados, usually those that are located in the vicinity of where people work and live. Since geography matters as to where people shop, geography matters as to where people gain access to in-store credit. Elizabeth, a thirty-seven-year-old seamstress at a local kite-surfing shop who was born and raised in the Callejón, discusses this common pattern:

I have a page in the cuadernos of two colmados: Colmado Junior, which I shop at when my husband or I come home from work in the afternoon, and Ana's, which is about a block from my house. I shop at Ana's early in the morning

Figure 3.4   Fiao Sign in Spanish. Photo taken by the author.

before I leave for work, or I send my oldest [daughter] there to pick something
up that I need to add to the mid-day meal before I return home.

There is a wide range as to how much debt residents incur among area colmados. Most residents who have access to in-store credit borrow between
20% and 50% of their monthly earnings. For example, Wilman, a thirty-
five-year-old Haitian gardener and handyman for two residences in ProCab,
shops at Pepe's and Rosalín's colmados. Pepe's is located in the same block
as Wilman's own house, and Rosalín's shop is on the way to the hardware
store near La Cienaga—a shop he frequents when he is sent on one of his
many daily errands from his employers. The Dominican minimum wage was
increased by 14% in July 2019 to approximately 11,600 pesos or US$265 a
month (Salario Mínimo 2019), yet many residents do not earn even close to
the minimum wage. Wilman does: his two part-time jobs pay a total of about
13,000 pesos a month. Wilman is allowed to secure a maximum debt of about
2,000 pesos in each colmado at any one time; if he accumulates the maximum
allowed debt in both colmados of 4,000 pesos—which he does each and every
month—he carries a monthly debt of about 31% of his monthly earnings.
Since debts are paid every two weeks, Wilman is required to pay Pepe and
Rosalín between 800 and 1,000 pesos each pay period. If he doesn't do so, or

if Wilman wants to accumulate more debt than the 2,000 peso maximum in each colmado, it is very likely that he will be turned down and will have to pay with cash for that purchase.

According to information gathered from all of my interviewees, the average debt residents accumulate per colmado is about 1,500 pesos (approximately US$34). But the median household debt is more telling of the population overall; in La Cienaga and the Callejón, the median household debt owed to any colmado is approximately 1,000 pesos (roughly US$23). And like Wilman, most residents incur the maximum allowed debt where they are given access to in-store credit. Shopkeepers and shoppers alike told me that it is expected that borrowers pay about 50% of their debt each quincenal. However, when asked, most residents reported that their typical quincenal payment is more apt to be about 25% to 30% of their accumulated debt. Shopkeepers anticipate this and budget accordingly.

When I inquired as to why shopkeepers would lend knowing that most borrowers at any one time pay down only 25% to 30% of their debt, they referred to fiao as a tool of attracting desirable customers. For example, Elías said, "Well, at least they're paying me something. As long as I budget for that, I'm ok. In fact, I really just need people to come into my store and buy. If they buy, I'm making money . . . . I'll get it [what is owed to me]." Rosalín's response shows a more direct link of fiao as a marketing tool: "If customers know that I will approve their purchase [give them fiao], then they will come to my store instead of some other store. The competition is tough . . . I have to do something to attract them to me." This is an important point: as discussed in chapter 2, colmados fix their prices; there are no sales or price-gouging. Therefore, one of the ways that colmados distinguish themselves from others is offering fiao to people who they want to return to their colmado. But as discussed in the next section, not all in-store credit is the same; these exchanges differ with respect to the people involved and to whom the expectation of repayment is made, if repayment is made at all.

THREE TYPES OF FIAO EXCHANGES

Overall, there are three types of fiao exchanges in colmados in Cabarete: (1) giving credit to someone who is known to pay it back, (2) gift-giving to someone in need so they won't go hungry, and (3) giving credit to someone who is not known as gente responsable.

The first, and most common, type of fiao exchange is one in which the shopkeeper knows and trusts the customer—a family member, neighbor, friend—to repay their debt, and therefore allows the person to buy on credit. Lozano (1997), in his research in Santo Domingo in the late 1980s, found that kin and family relations, both family members who had migrated abroad and those who still lived in the Dominican Republic, were key to provisioning households. But in Cabarete, a place where people migrate to, instead of from (as in the case of family members in Lozano's study who migrated from Santo Domingo to New York or Miami), fiao creates social ties between and among people who often are not kin, and these social ties become key components of their strategies to provision the household. Stronger than the close social tie is the fact that the customer is known to "have a job." "Having a job" was a phrase used by all shopkeepers in interviews with me and is a key factor in delineating who is gente responsable. However, knowing as I do that most residents in El Callejón and La Cienaga work in the unpredictable tourist industry, I questioned shopkeepers about how they knew if their customers would continue to have jobs when it was time to pay off their debts. "I don't," said Jhonny, a Dominican shopkeeper in La Cienaga. "But I have to hope that he knows someone who could help him pay me in that situation." Jhonny's comment demonstrates that it is common practice to make small loans to family members or friends so that when they need a loan, they can rely on those to whom they've loaned money in the past. I asked Jhonny if he had given fiao to people who were known to be gente responsable, but then were not able to pay off their debt and needed to borrow from others to do so. He acknowledged that indeed this happens but doesn't concern him: as long as customers pay their debt, he doesn't care from where or whom the money comes.

In every interview with shopkeepers, they discussed the circle of debt, or the role that customers' debt repayment plays in the financial health of colmados. Unprompted by me, shopkeepers provided me with many stories of colmados that had gone into financial ruin and closed because of failed debt repayment. "Not only do I have people who owe me money," reported Isayis, "but I owe the distributors money. When customers don't pay me back, I can't pay my bills, and my business suffers." Distributors have fiao notebooks documenting shopkeepers' debt, just as shopkeepers have to record their customers' debts. If customers fail to repay their debts, then shopkeepers can't pay their own debts. Isayis' statement above alludes to the fact that for the most part, the local fiao system of socioeconomic exchange is fragile. Like micro-loans made in other cultural settings (e.g., Karim 2008), the system can only maintain itself if people at all levels, distributors, shopkeepers, and customers, are gente responsable.

There is a second type of fiao exchange that has nothing to do with gente responsable. In fact, by definition, these exchanges specifically take place with people who are not responsible. Sometimes, a resident of the community comes to a shopkeeper and asks for a gift. These residents do not work or haven't worked for some time, and they use this request as their last resort: they've burned other bridges, such as with family and friends, because they've failed to repay loans. "Usually," said Anouz, a Haitian shopkeeper in El Callejón, "this person is hungry and needs me to help him . . . or their kids would go hungry." Anouz illustrated this further with a story about a woman who came to her to ask for items, such as disposable diapers, milk, and eggs, for herself and her infant. Anouz knew in this case that she was giving a gift that would never be repaid. I asked her how often she did this, and she said that she gives these types of gifts only once to a person who asks. Often, shopkeepers refer to their religious/spiritual beliefs as Catholics or Christians in order to explain their gift-giving. "I'm a believer [in God] and this is what he wants me to do [looking up and pointing at the sky]," explained Anouz. Josué, another shopkeeper, stated that "if we give too many gifts, our colmado would without a doubt fall [into financial ruin]."

In every case, when I asked shopkeepers how they know who or who isn't gente responsable, they replied, "people who pay their debts," with a strange look on their faces, as if I failed to understand the objective of financial transactions. However, when I pushed them to further delineate how they might be able to distinguish responsible people when they first meet someone, then they answer, as did Anouz: "Ah, when that happens, I ask for a reference, someone who I know who can vouch for them as responsible people." Anouz's response details the third type of fiao exchange: in cases when shopkeepers get a request for fiao from someone they don't know, it is common practice for the prospective customer to bring a person with them, a reference, to vouch for their character. The reference tells the shopkeeper two things: (1) that the person has financial income coming from somewhere and can be trusted to pay their debt, and (2) that the reference will allow the shopkeeper to put the total amount borrowed in their own—the reference's, not the shopper's—debt column in the fiao notebooks. The function of this third type of fiao exchange is crucial, indebting the borrower to the reference, not the shopkeeper. If the borrower fails to pay the debt, then the reference is responsible to pay that debt. This, in fact, mitigates the risk to the shopkeeper. This third category of fiao encourages social networking among residents who are looking for responsible people upon whom they can rely for future help. The expected fiao practice of vouching for someone until a person can prove themselves responsible demonstrates the importance of social networks among customers, as well as between customers and shopkeepers.

Building on Mauss' (1966) work on gift exchanges as sets of practices which create and bind the social ties between givers and receivers, Peebles (2010, 226) contends that "credit and debt stand as an inseparable, dyadic unit." This is exemplified in the Callejón and La Cienaga, where everyone who uses fiao has in turn vouched for others to be eligible for in-store credit. In other words, everyone who is a borrower has also been a creditor, an individual who extends credit to another so that the person they vouch for can, eventually, become gente responsable. Because most people in these neighborhoods use fiao to provision their households, most residents are borrower/creditors.

Although most residents in La Cienaga and El Callejón use fiao to some extent, not everyone claims that they should. Incurring debt in neighborhood colmados is a morally charged process, invoking a range of reactions— sometimes very strong reactions—from residents, just like Amelia did in the vignette at the beginning of this chapter when she indicated that having access to in-store credit is "for dignity" (pa' la dignidad). When discussing fiao, residents provide moral justification and judgments not only about cus- tomers using in-store credit, but also about shopkeepers giving or withhold- ing fiao to customers. Far from just an economic practice, culturally salient perceptions of fiao in Cabarete revolve around conceptions of care (for the self, family, and others) and mitigating risk (both the risk of not provisioning the household and the risk of debt non-repayment). All shoppers had at least one story of being denied fiao at a colmado—in other words, being deemed unworthy—when the customer felt they should have been offered fiao. And at the same time, every colmadero had stories of making the decision—some- times split-second decisions—of determining who is or isn't gente respon- sable. Just as Graeber has pointed out more generally around the world, the ability to incur debt and/or make loans in the Callejón and La Cienaga has become intimately "tied up with conceptions of moral personhood" (Graeber 2011, 390).

EMERGENT MORALITIES OF DEBT IN CABARETE

Like shopping, the moral experiences of living with debt have garnered ethnographic attention, particularly after the Great Recession of 2008. Ross (2013) argues that within this social context he considers a "creditocracy," indebtedness has become ubiquitous and necessary among those aspiring to and maintaining their position in the middle class, even to the point of financ- ing everyday basic goods—as has occurred in the context of food shopping among the working poor in the Dominican Republic. Within creditocracies, Stout (2016) contends that moralizing discourses have evolved around the obligation of debt repayment. But after the Great Recession, Jefferson (2013) found people living through and by this moral experience, critiqued their obligation to repay, and as echoed by Zigon and Throop (2014), reinterpreted this obligation, and repositioned themselves by walking away from their debt, citing corporate greed and government ineptitude as justification for their non-repayment. As Roitman (2005, 12) points out, the morality of debt can mediate different "forms of sociality" as people make sense of their own positions within varying social imaginaries. Discourses of debt—whether to accumulate debt, to pay it back, or to allow others to borrow—create emergent moralities[1] that define the boundaries of these experiences. Emergent moralities, therefore, are historically and culturally contextual values and judgments that evolve to help people rethink, reinterpret, reimagine, and reposition themselves as, what Zigon and Throop (2014, 8) note, "sufferers or actors" within a particular social environment. In Cabarete, fiao has become a mediated form of sociality as working-class residents finance food and other basic necessities in colmados to survive, generating emergent moralities as a result.

People's developing conceptions of debt have produced a variety of emergent moralities outside of the Dominican Republic. For example, in Santiago, Chile, García-Grandon (2019) found that women use credit cards as tools to care for their families by mitigating the risks leading to household food insecurity. Supermarkets have expanded household credit among low-income populations, offering credit cards to customers, primarily women, who are able to pay off their debts in a preselected number of installments. Supermarkets have become the primary credit-giving institution among the working poor in a context of very low salaries, sparse government help, and precarious working conditions, a context not unlike Cabarete. García-Grandon's interviewees articulated emergent moralities for their indebtedness that revolve around an axis of blame. They use moral frames which envision themselves as consumers who are responsible for their own self-care, a subjectivity originating from neoliberal discourse so pervasive in Chile since the 1970s (see Paley 2001). Some women blamed themselves, what García-Grandon calls the "at-fault frame," for their experiences of incurring more debt than they could repay. Attributing their indebtedness to a failure of character and lack of organization, these subjects positioned themselves and others as incurring debt to satiate desires that they might well—and should—live without; for example, one woman spoke of how her uncle financed goods like salami, cheese, and cakes, inferring that since these products were not staples, they should be avoided and not financed. Other subjects clearly indicated that they were not at fault for their indebtedness, stating that their lines of credit were the only things allowing them to provision their households, even if they were unable to meet their repayment goals. And finally, García-Grandon asserts that another group of subjects remained ambivalent on the matter of debt. While they did indeed claim pervasive indebtedness among the working class, they were reluctant to lay blame on either shoppers or supermarkets, instead explaining the emerging trend of increased indebtedness because of low-income shoppers' lack of financial knowledge or as an inherent part of hegemonic consumerism.

These new emergent moralities are significant because they illustrate that perpetual indebtedness is not only a middle-class norm. As has occurred in Santiago, the creditocracy has seeped into everyday life for the working poor in Cabarete as well. Fiao, not credit cards, ensures that people can provision their households in Cabarete, but at the mercy of col-maderos who may or may not allow customers to buy on credit. Emergent moralities of fiao among residents of the Callejón and La Cienaga involve perceptions of fiao related to borrowers and creditors: borrowers who are both shoppers and shopkeepers, and creditors who are shoppers, shop-keepers, and distributors. When discussing fiao, residents of the Callejón and La Cienaga speak of it in moral terms, often referring to blame. But the blame that is cast is contingent, spanning a range of perceptions based upon who is borrowing and from whom they are borrowing, who is lend-ing and to whom they are lending, and how this debt is situated within the very fragile moral economy.

Being Gente Responsable: Dignity, Trust, Taking Care of Others, and Hard Work

Like Amelia in the vignette that began this chapter, most people view fiao as their lifeline to provisioning their households. Out of the forty inter-viewees in the Callejón and La Cienaga, thirty-four people, 85% of my interviewees, used the phrase, "pa' la dignidad," indicating that garnering in-store credit to buy food in colmados gives them "dignity." Residents in Cabarete who connect fiao to dignity refer to their own vulnerability and understand their place within the local economy that makes money at their expense. Like many defaulted homeowners in Detroit (Jefferson 2013), residents of the Callejón and La Cienaga are astutely aware of their exploitation; while living and working in Cabarete, it is easy to see the stark differences between their own lives and the lives of not only tourists but also middle-class residents—those who are working-class residents' managers, supervisors, and directors.

Rita, a twenty-four-year-old mother of two young girls, moved to Cabarete with her older brother, Leo, when she was fourteen. Leo bought a used motor-cycle in his hometown, San Francisco de Macorís, when he was seventeen, and the man who sold it to him told him that there was good money to be made in Cabarete as a motorcycle taxi driver. Now, ten years later, he has paid off his motorcycle, giving him more monthly income than he previously had, which contributes to paying household expenses for the four of them: Rita, her two daughters, and Leo. Rita cleans houses three days a week in nearby residences located in the neighborhoods of ProCab, East Cabarete, and Pista Motocross. When asked about fiao, Rita explains,

I have no security here . . . Leo's job is more secure because he has more senior-ity and is likeable. Many people [tourists] call him to take them places, and with that he'll get a full day's pay. But when there are fewer tourists, he gets just enough to pay for a little rice, some beans, sometimes we pick an avocado [from a tree nearby] or someone gives us a plantain. When Edwin gives us our in-store credit, we buy more, we have chicken. But I know the people I work for always have chicken . . . I am paid so little. Sometimes Leo drops me off [at work] with my girls, just so that my employer can see what I need money for. [CH: Have you ever asked for a raise? Did you get it?] Ha . . . I get the typical rate, Cristina, we have no security here. We have no security here except what we make for ourselves, making sure that we have fiao.

Like Rita, many residents state that fiao gives them security. Darwin is an ambulant jewelry seller on the beaches of Cabarete and has been living in La Cienaga for the last twelve of his thirty-eight years. His briefcase full of neck-laces, rings, and bracelets made with shells, amber, and larimar (semiprecious stones mined in the Dominican Republic) usually earns him, on average, about 100 pesos a day, and sometimes, during the high tourist season and with a little luck, he might bring home 1,000 pesos a day, "but that's not typical, I can't count on that," he told me. His household of six consists of his wife, Demariy, his two school-age children who attend a nearby private school on a partial scholarship, and two other family members he is caring for: his aging aunt and the twelve-year-old daughter of his oldest brother. "I am given a tab at Edwin's and Rosalín's colmados for most of the year," Darwin reported. "I work hard, and they [Edwin and Rosalín] know that. Without fiao, I have no security, I can't feed my family. Fiao gives us dignity."

Residents who see fiao as a path to dignity also talk about debt repayment. "I need to pay my tab, that's dignity, that's being responsible," Ramona, a twenty-three-year-old food server in a nearby restaurant, told me. "Paying back my debt shows Ana and Edwin [colmaderos in the Callejón where Ramona shops] that I can be trusted." There are times when she is unable to pay her debt, especially from late August to November, so colmaderos start to deny her a line of credit until she repays all of her debt. It is important to Ramona that she is considered gente responsable, even when she is unable to pay her debt and is denied fiao. The phrase, "I work hard," or referring to themselves as "hardworking" (*trabajador/a*) was part of most interviews that I conducted. It was used not only by customers but also by colmaderos. Because being gente responsable is synonymous with "having a job," being afforded a line of credit in a colmado signifies shopkeepers' trust that the shopper works hard. And colmaderos are known as hardworking when they try to maintain shoppers' fiao even in the face of little debt repayment or no debt repayment. Ramona explains, "Even when I can't repay my debt, Ana and Edwin . . . they wait a long time to deny me fiao, they work hard to avoid that [denying me], but I know they don't blame me. They know . . . it's not *my* fault" [Ramona's emphasis].

Like Ramona when she is unable to pay her debt, Rosa absolves herself of any blame, instead laying blame at the foot of others who she considers more responsible for her exploitation: "[The hotel where she works] makes so much money . . . they could afford to pay me more . . . but they don't. It's not my fault when I can't pay my debt . . . I work hard but I can't get ahead [*pa'lante*]." When I asked Rosa whose fault it is, she says, "it's my boss who won't pay me more . . . it's all of our bosses. That's just the way it is. These are the rules."

Shakow (2019) describes the emergent morality of an aspiring new middle class in Bolivia and the complexity of *salir adelante*, or getting ahead under the direction of former president Evo Morales and his political party, MAS (Movement Toward Socialism). With his presidential election in 2005, Morales' promotion of social equality and the redistribution of wealth shifted the local landscape of what constitutes getting ahead, particularly with regard to high educational attainment, becoming a professional, and patterns of material consumption. In that social milieu, new understandings evolved as to who works hard and who should gain entrée to professional and political positions, a defining feature of the middle class. But in the Dominican Republic, the phrase "pa'lante" is often used to signify just getting by[2] or what is reminiscent of the way Zigon (2007) describes "the struggles of actual individuals who must wake up each day and make efforts to 'keep going'" (quoted in Zigon and Throop 2014). In effect, Rosa's hard work does not elicit any change in status; it helps her to just get by so she can keep going, but it fails to translate into any kind of entrée into the middle class. Fiao for Rosa is part of the struggle even inasmuch as it is part of a financial strategy to maintain some dignity in her life.

While most interviewees told me that it was not their own fault when they are unable to repay their debts, only some of them laid the blame somewhere else, as Rosa did when she blamed her place of employment or "the rules." But interestingly, when they did refer to blame, only one interviewee blamed colmaderos for denying customers in-store credit. Overall, residents showed me that they understand colmaderos have debts, too, and that these debts are linked to customer repayment. Customers' knowledge of this did not surprise me because typically when colmaderos deny fiao to customers, especially gente responsable, they often do so by reminding them that colmaderos are unable to pay their own debts when customer debt isn't paid up. Edwin and his ayudantes in the Callejón repeatedly tell customers that "if you don't pay, I can't pay, and I have to pay to stay open," meaning that to keep his colmado solvent, he needs to pay his bills. Instead of maintaining distance between themselves and their customers using mechanisms of othering, as Wynne (2014) found between Dominicans and Haitians in Monte Cristi, shopkeepers in the Callejón and La Cienaga use idioms of solidarity or phrases that remind customers that they have a responsibility to pay their debts so that colmaderos can pay their own bills.

"A Gift Is Not Always a Gift, You Know": Personal Failure, Overspending, and Neglecting the Individual

Although far less frequently expressed by my interviewees, another moralizing discourse of fiao is emerging in the context of Cabarete, one that implicates shoppers and shopkeepers for their perpetual indebtedness because of their focus on taking care of others instead of focusing on individual responsibility and financial self-care. Four interviewees in the Callejón and two in La Cienaga view fiao in this unfavorable light. All of them were evangelical Christians, but not all evangelical Christians who were interviewed viewed fiao the way these six individuals did.

Aryceli was born in the Callejón and runs a small non-profit organization, which garners her just enough to make a lower-middle-class income for her household consisting of her husband and her four children. She and her husband are active members of the Dominican Christian church in the Callejón. When asked about fiao, Aryceli and her husband told me that they always shop at colmados with money. They proudly reported that, in all their time living and working in the Callejón, they never had a page in any notebooks at colmados. Is that because you don't need fiao to get by week after week? I asked them. Aryceli replied,

> We struggle, maybe not as much as the other people here [in the Callejón], but we don't have a lot. But it is certain that we have more than most people. I think that fiao makes people dependent. It makes them slaves to colmados. [CH: But what if they can't eat without fiao?] That's not true! They buy too much, they don't need everything they buy. [CH: Can you give me an example?] Yes, Oscar . . . he goes to Josué's every night and opens a tab, and then Abril [his wife] has to work harder to pay it, braiding more hair.

According to Aryceli, people who use fiao are at fault and to blame for overspending or wrongly spending on purchases she deems unfit, such as putting alcohol consumption on a tab, like Oscar does at a well-known colmadón. Not only that, Aryceli indicates that because of their husbands' transgressions, women are the ones who suffer and have to work harder, as does Oscar's wife, Abril, who provides braiding and other hair services to customers at the beach. Sometimes men do indeed incur debt at colmadones, where they put drinks or bottles of rum or beer on a tab, but it is not the norm. When I asked them directly, only two people discussed men running up tabs drinking at colmadones as a factor that maintained perpetual household indebtedness.

Perceiving fiao as a personal failure, especially in the sense of not being able to get ahead, was a common theme for these six interviewees. Their sentiments were tinged with blame for what they alleged was people's seeming lack of focus on their own needs. Not unlike other settings in Latin America in which evangelical Christianity has promoted alternative visions of "hard work" and the individual neoliberal subject (e.g., Girard 2019; Adams 2019), this emergent morality of fiao identifies the obligations borrowers have to each other as an inherent part of the problem. Instead of viewing indebtedness as an intrinsic part of hegemonic consumerism, as did some of García-Grandon's subjects who reframed their use of credit cards to purchase food in Chile, my interviewees indicate that, far from being a gift to assist them with provisioning their households, fiao entraps borrowers and obligates them to incur more and more debt. "When fiao is used, people don't think about themselves, to work to get ahead, instead they have to take care of others and for that, they get trapped. A gift is not always a gift, you know?" Sonia asked me, as way of explanation.

It is not coincidental that the emergent morality of fiao as personal failure is being established by those residents who consider themselves as part of the very small middle class in the Callejón and La Cienaga. Anthropologists, such as Sherry Ortner in her work in New Jersey (2003) and Maureen O'Dougherty in her ethnography of Brazil (2002), show us the shifting and contested quality of the middle class and the ways in which moral boundaries are drawn around categories of people who belong and those who do not. Analysis of people's lived experiences of the middle class in different contexts demonstrates that this coveted category is something that is simultaneously aspired to but fiercely defended by those who are designated as such. Ortner calls this "class as a project," a process of distinguishing between oneself and those who are poorer and using moral explanations for one's success. For residents in the Callejón and La Cienaga, consumption patterns are a marker of class, laden with moral overtones. For residents who use this emergent morality of blame, using fiao is a sign of contributing to the reproduction of poverty and therefore not belonging to the middle class.

For two of the interviewees who articulated this emergent morality, fiao was both lauded and vilified in the same breadth. Josué, a thirty-four-year-old Haitian resident who moved to the Callejón in 2014, belongs to the Haitian Christian church in the Callejón and is an active member of the men's choir. Josué argues that while he desperately needs fiao, he looks forward to the day when he doesn't need it. "We don't eat without fiao. But fiao obliges me to allow other people to put their debt under my name in Edwin's notebook," he explains. "It's exhausting." A long-time Dominican resident of Cabarete who lives in La Cienaga, Joaquin, describes the hold fiao has over him:

> I need fiao, it helps me and my family. But it also hurts us. I have had many neighbors ask me to vouch for them, so they put their debt on my own [page in the notebook]. They pay off their debt, but not quickly enough, so that my own debt appears so large . . . then, shopkeepers have denied me in-store credit because they think I have overspent, when really, it's because my debt was partly another person's debt. But when this happens, usually I explain this to shopkeepers . . . I help them realize that I bring in more shoppers, and then sometimes they leave me alone [let me pay continue paying with fiao].

Joaquin's experiences highlight the importance of the role of colmaderos. Colmaderos are the fulcrum around which fiao pivots: to achieve a successful business, shopkeepers must give in-store credit to customers, but if they lend too often to people who are unable to repay their debts, they can do a disservice to themselves and the community. However, colmaderos quite often allow people to buy food on credit even when they are unable to repay, either in part or in full.

COLMADEROS: PROFESSIONALS "JUST GETTING BY"

The effects of debt non-repayment on the financial solvency of local colmados is further detailed in chapter 4, yet this is relevant to the emergent moralities of fiao and how shopkeepers make sense of their obligations to care for others and the risk they take on when doing so. Colmaderos also have a role to play in people's conceptions of being responsible, one that encompasses care for others by extending in-store credit. Working hard to be responsible as shopkeepers means that they have a responsibility to the community as well as to their colmados. They use the phrase "to be professional" (*ser profesional*) to indicate that shopkeepers play an important part in their communities, in no small measure for helping people to provision their households and for the jobs they create within their communities.

Typically, to be a professional in the Dominican Republic is linked to the middle class. But in the case of colmaderos, it is debatable as to whether being a shopkeeper allows for entrée into the middle class. There is a professional organization comprised of colmaderos in the Dominican Republic called *Federación Nacional de Comerciantes Detallistas de Provisiones*, or the National Federation of Retailer of Provisions (known by the acronym, FENACODEP). Since its founding in 1976, this organization consists of over 30,000 members throughout the country and works to "promote the development and modernization of colmados and its institutional structure" (FENACODEP 2019). Member benefits include access to medical, business, and vehicle insurance; savings and credit accounts through regional banks; and training and loans through a national program called PRODIPYME, the program for Micro-, Small-, and Medium-Sized Enterprises (United Nations Social and Economic Council 2008). FENACODEP publishes a newspaper that is also available online called *El Detallista* (The Retailer) and maintains a weekly television show called *Detallista y Globalización* (Retail and Globalization). Additionally, this professional organization organizes an annual conference in Santo Domingo and partners with other national programs and professionals of interest to its members, such as the annual festival for Micro-, Small-, and Medium-Sized Enterprises, an organization which includes but is not exclusive to colmados. FENACODEP serves as the collective voice of small business owners and uses this voice to advocate for business-friendly policies and regulations at the national and local levels. As such, FENACODEP promotes a professional culture, with all of the signs and signals of financial security: access to credit, loans, banking, insurance, and training, as well as social networking and social media.

But in everyday life, the role of shopkeeper is a precarious one, especially in the Callejón and La Cienaga. Of the twelve neighborhood colmaderos who I encountered in my day-to-day research, only three were familiar with FENACODEP, and only one of them had been an active FENACODEP member. These three colmaderos had received PRODIMYPE loans when they first opened their colmados, but they have never received medical or vehicle insurance or any kind of formal credit beyond the fiao they receive from their distributors. All twelve colmaderos incur a tremendous amount of debt to their distributors to keep their shelves stocked. Many colmaderos do not draw distinctions between themselves and their customers because of the burden they have of keeping their colmados afloat. Although colmaderos are small business owners, and therefore professionals, shopkeepers in the Callejón and La Cienaga find it difficult to get ahead, instead using the same phrase "pa'lante" to characterize and signify their shared vulnerability with customers of "just getting by." Most shopkeepers told me that they are expected to "sacrifice" for the good of their customers. For example, Ana indicates that to keep her colmado alive, she depends upon shoppers who come back to her shop, even when they can't pay.

My customers are poor people, Cristina . . . I know, I am one of them, I'm poor too [laughs]! I need to keep them coming back, so I make sure that I budget for low debt repayment during the lean months [when tourism slows]. [CH: How much do you budget for?] Well, I try to push as far as I can . . . sometimes I know that I can't make what I owe, so I have to beg distributors not to cut me off [from their own lines of credit with distributors]. Maybe each quincenal I collect 10% of what I'm owed. And that's when my shop has fewer products to buy . . . I have to slow down buying inventory. That's the sacrifice that I have to make . . . I don't make much money as a shopkeeper, but I have to sacrifice for my customers. But most distributors take care of me, so I can take care of my customers. [CH: How do they do that? What do you mean?] They [distributors] don't cut me off, so I don't cut off my customers. Or I just don't order much when I can't pay my own debts.

Additionally, Ana's insight exposes one of the limits of fiao: although fiao is an important feature of just getting by in Cabarete, it does not curb poverty for shoppers or shopkeepers.

David, a thirty-seven-year-old driver who lives in Sosúa and works for a beverage distribution company, understands the fragility of the system, especially in his work in neighborhoods like the Callejón and La Cienaga. In his ten years working with the same company, David sees ebbs and flows to his deliveries. "I don't even know what the Callejón is like in October, I barely make deliveries then [laughs]. Well, sometimes I go there [during slow periods of tourism], but I don't do much business. They [shopkeepers] just can't pay up." When I asked him how often colmaderos fail to repay their debts, David reported that he is authorized to allow late repayment twice, and since he makes weekly deliveries, this means colmaderos have a two-week grace period. After that, "I can't take anything off the motorcycle," David told me, meaning that if the colmadero fails to pay their debt that week, he will not unload the delivery from his motorcycle and will take it back to the distribution center.

For colmaderos, taking care of customers by allowing them to purchase on credit, even when customers are unable to repay, is afforded when distributors take care of them. The predominant emergent morality of fiao is one in which, in no small measure, people need to work hard to take care of each other, even at some risk to themselves. In so doing, shopkeepers hope to carry themselves through hard times. They take this risk in anticipation that one of their shoppers may return to work for a tourist who is coming into town the next week or a local kite-boarding shop might have a group coming in the off-season to take advantage of the cheaper rates. These kinds of contingencies determine whether or not colmaderos can pay distributors, stock their shelves, and thereby extend offers of credit to their customers.

CONCLUSION

Emergent moralities of fiao in Cabarete mediate people's perceptions of their obligations to care for themselves and others, as well as their

Figure 3.5   Distributor Making Delivery. Photo taken by the author.

ability to mitigate the risk of provisioning households and working toward financial solvency. All three types of fiao are predicated upon relationships between themselves, other shoppers, and shopkeepers. Fiao is never guaranteed and is always a product of assessing the borrower's place within local economic conditions. Most residents cast fiao as a strategy to preserve dignity and enhance their household security, but they also recognize that using fiao is not a route out of poverty. There is an undercurrent of blame among some residents who frame borrowers as culpable for their own perpetual indebtedness.

Emergent moralities articulate with changing social, economic, political, and cultural conditions in context. This chapter has illustrated what it means to be gente responsable and how being responsible changes in relation to competing emergent moralities: for most, being responsible means debt repayment, giving in-store credit, and helping others secure fiao, and for a few people, being responsible means taking care of the self, not borrowing, and spending only what is earned. The next chapter examines the hidden work of borrower/creditor fiao exchanges and the role that this hidden work has, not as part of the concept of *being* responsible, but in the process of *becoming* gente responsable.

NOTES

1. I am grateful to Miriam Shakow, co-chair of a panel in which I participated at the 2019 Latin American Studies Association meetings in Boston, Massachusetts, for her coining of the phrase "emergent moralities," in post-conference correspondence.

2. Garth (2020) found that, in Cuba, the phrase *luchando la vida*, meaning "just getting by," also has a metaphorical meaning to signify acquiring food through the black market. Although pa'lante also means "just getting by," it has no relevance to the black market in the Dominican Republic.

Chapter 4

"The Door Is Always Open . . . Until It Isn't"

The Hidden Labor of Becoming Gente Responsable

3 October 2014

Pepe's corner store is in the heart of the Callejón, located at a major intersection where a side-road forks, serving people living on both arteries running through this residential district. His is one of the most popular colmados in the Callejón, and arguably one of the most frequented in all of Cabarete. Even when I first started working in Cabarete, it was easy to spot Pepe: a 60-year old Dominican man and a lifelong resident of the Callejón, who typically worked shirtless, with salt and pepper, short, cropped hair and a wide smile. "I've lived here long before the Callejón was as big as it is now," he explained. He lives nearby the colmado, and each day I often found him sitting outside or across the street from the store in the requisite white plastic chair so ubiquitous throughout the Dominican Republic. Interestingly, Pepe infrequently works inside his colmado; the only times he was seen working in the colmado was when he butchered animals made to order for customers, a role he saw fit for only himself, or sometimes to go over the purchase orders from distributors or accounts of customers' debt. Those who typically worked behind the counter and at the register were young men in their late teens, like Manuel, a 19 year old single Dominican and lifelong resident of the Callejón, who was working this morning when I arrived at 7:15. Along with Manuel, this morning Pepe was in the colmado, too; when I arrived, he was in the later stages of butchering a chicken for a customer who had made the order by phone. After finishing the meat order, Pepe gestured to me—in pure Dominican fashion, with lips scrunched up to the side of his face, a quick nod of his head, eyebrows raised—first looking at me and then over to the plastic chairs outside the colmado. We made our way over, across the road about 15 meters away from the colmado, to sit in the shade and talk. My questions

107

for him today were all about how and why he allowed particular customers to buy food on credit.

"The door is always opened for responsible people," said Pepe, "you know, those who I know will pay me." I've heard this phrase—"siempre la puerta está abierta," or the door is always opened—often from other shop- keepers as they talk to or about their most trusted customers. Pepe means this metaphorically and perhaps a bit literally as well, since colmaderos are known to get phone calls in the middle of the night from customers need- ing emergency supplies. "I need these customers—I have debts, you know? If these responsible people don't shop here, they'll shop somewhere else. I would be ruined. I work hard to keep the door open for them."

In response, I asked him, "When is the door not opened for someone? How do you know that someone will pay you back?"

"Oh yes, the door closes, that's for sure [Ah sí, la puerta se cierra, es cierto]," Pepe replied. "I can't give everyone credit. If I did, I can't pay my own debts because there are lazy people here, those who don't work, and they are thieves and wouldn't pay me back."

"But what about people who only work during tourist seasons? Are they lazy? Do you allow them to buy on credit when there are no tourists?" I asked.

"Well, my friend, yes, this is a problem . . .. For these people, they are responsible people when they are able to be. But more than anything, I'm talking about the Haitians. I can't trust them."

"So you mean like Joel? And Esther? How about Robe? It appears to me that you lend to Haitians quite a bit," I pushed him.

"Well, yeah, I do, but they're not like other Haitians."

"Like who? What do you mean?" I asked.

"Well, I suppose they [Joel, Esther, and Robe] have become gente respon- sable, they prove that to me," was Pepe's explanation.

"Are Haitian customers the only ones who are not responsible, who fail to pay their debts? Do Dominicans do that, too, or is it just Haitians?" I asked.

"No, you're right, there are Dominicans, too," conceded Pepe. "The door is always open, Cristina, until it isn't, you know?"

"The door" that Pepe mentioned not only refers to the relationship between the specific customer and shopkeeper who are engaging in the specific trans- action, but also to the networks that fiao creates by weaving together people who vouch for each other. The door is opened only for customers who can find gente responsable to vouch for them. Shopkeepers want particular customers to return to shop at their store, and to do so, they woo desir- able shoppers with the promise of making purchases using in-store credit. Throughout my fieldwork, I found comments like Pepe's to be very common among colmaderos. In fact, I had a dozen such interactions with shopkeepers, conversations in which they would complain to me that Haitians could not be trusted, but I had firsthand knowledge of them extending credit to Haitians who in fact repaid their debt on their own accord or with the help of other *gente responsable*. When I confronted colmaderos with these anecdotes, they would then turn around and admit to me that they never, or close to never, withheld fiao from Haitians.

Murray (1996, 238) indicates that in communities with many colmados, like Cabarete, there is fierce competition to attract desirable customers, and *"el truco es saber a quien fiar* [the trick is knowing to whom to give fiao]" (Murray 1996, 256), alluding to the capacity colmaderos must develop in order to maintain the solvency of their shops and to stay in business. Yet Murray's work does little to reveal "the trick" colmaderos use to distinguish responsible people from those who fail to repay their debts. In this chapter, I discuss this trick and build upon my discussion in chapter 3 about the third type of fiao exchange, what I call "borrower/creditor exchanges": when a person is called upon to take on another person's debt, someone who must be vouched for because they are a customer who is either unknown to the shopkeeper or someone who is temporarily unemployed. Borrower/creditor exchanges mitigate the risk to the shopkeeper of extending credit. It is a previously undocumented phenomenon and one that fundamentally creates networks of people, often including intercultural relationships, who residents can count on in times of need. In this way, buying food on credit reveals a moral economy that functions as a social safety net, regardless of prejudicial perceptions of the Other that may or may not be transcended when engaging in fiao. For Dominicans, Haitians, and Dominico-Haitians who work in the vulnerable economy of Cabarete, they need people they can count on, and this need is prioritized above and beyond their need to create mechanisms of othering between themselves and others. In fact, intercultural engagement between Dominicans and Haitians is the norm, not the exception, for food shopping in Cabarete. Dominicans and Haitians may use rhetoric of intercultural distrust, but colmados are spaces where people's shared responses to increasing economic hardships often transcend typical, long-standing prejudice and discrimination along social constructions of race. In colmados in El Callejón and La Cienaga, this type of fiao exchange becomes a process of negotiating, contesting, and remaking boundaries of who can mitigate risk, drawing distinctions between people who have the resources necessary to help at a given moment in time. What this looks like in everyday life is that people can and do harbor racist ideas while simultaneously extending fiao to those who are the target of these racist ideas.

Shoppers are not the only ones who count on fiao to buy food. In fact, colmaderos depend on fiao to purchase food from distributors who deliver inventory to their establishments. At times, shoppers fail to pay not only their debts to colmaderos but also the debts that others have incurred on their behalf. Additionally, shopkeepers sometimes fail to repay their own debts to distributors. In these ways, credit and debt are intricately intertwined; if people give credit to shoppers who fail to repay their debts, shopkeepers will not consider them responsible and deny them fiao. Further, if shopkeepers give in-store credit to too many people who fail to repay their loans, the risk of bankruptcy increases for the colmadero. "The door is always open until it isn't," although meant metaphorically to represent the door of in-store credit, it also has the quite literal meaning of colmados' doors closing forever due to bankruptcy. This is what Sonia meant, at the end of chapter 3, when she said, "A gift is not always a gift, you know?" The irony is that, while essential for provisioning households and colmados, extending the gift of credit can result in both household food insecurity for shoppers and financial ruin for colmaderos.

While chapter 3 elucidates what *being* gente responsable means, I turn now to the complex process of *becoming* gente responsable, or the hidden labor in which people engage to create social relationships in the Callejón and La Cienaga to help them provision their households. These social relationships intersect with local perceptions of race/ethnicity, gender, and class. Being gente responsable is an abstract concept with cultural salience in Cabarete; in other words, everyone knows what is meant when they say that the key to buying food on credit is by "being a responsible person." But being considered gente responsable is not a status that is fixed, permanent, or ascribed. A person who is distinguished as gente responsable in one shopping encounter can often be considered not responsible in another. Becoming gente responsable is a process of hidden and productive labor that is fostered and developed in the Callejón and La Cienaga because of everyday contact with the Other. This chapter illustrates the fragility of fiao, the effects of its failure on different actors (shoppers and shopkeepers), and the strategies individuals use in the Callejón and La Cienaga to cope with the fragility of fiao, such as sharing food and meals.

THE HIDDEN LABOR OF CREDIT AND DEBT

In a summative article about the anthropology of credit and debt, Peebles (2010, 234) notes that "the ethnographic task over many years has been to study how the credit/debt nexus is productive of social ties, allegiances, enmities, and hostilities, rather than to make normative pronouncements concerning whether credit is liberating and debt is debilitating." In the last chapter, we saw that residents of Cabarete have developed emerging moralities of fiao that account for culturally significant understandings of hard work and caring for others who are in the same or near-similar circumstances. Most residents consider fiao, both lending and receiving in-store credit, to be a process that incorporates empathy for others, working hard to find ways to help others in need, and making sure that others do not go without. This hard work is not without self-interest: residents are keenly aware that lending in-store credit or vouching so that others can receive in-store credit are important ways of ensuring that they themselves can count on others in times of need. In Cabarete, fiao as a process can be both liberating and debilitating, but more importantly, it is a process of creating social safety nets, often through intercultural, Dominican-Haitian relationships. Yet the hard work of creating these social safety nets has not been accounted for in the literature on colmados in the Dominican Republic nor in the literature on Haitian-Dominican relations. My work in the Callejón and La Cienaga exposes the limits of the fatal-conflict model of Hispaniola that assumes strained Dominican-Haitian interpersonal relations and shows that people are astutely aware of the benefits they accrue from engaging in intercultural fiao exchanges.

In other cultural and economic contexts, anthropologists have studied what Peebles (2010, 229) calls the "socialization of debt" or the process and its effects of creating social ties between and among creditors and borrowers. Most of these cross-cultural ethnographic examples examine the social practices that develop from micro-credit lending and borrowing, especially the collective obligations women borrowers have to each other to repay these loans—a well-known, universal micro-loan practice first established through organizations like the Grameen Bank in Bangladesh (Karim 2011; Grameen 2019). In micro-credit organizations, if women default on their loans, typically other borrowers become responsible for repaying the defaulted debt, an occasion that women work hard to avoid. Hayes (2017), for example, examines the hidden and productive labor of women microenterprise vendors as they manage and repay micro-loan debts in northern Honduras. She found that borrowers are often engaged in multiple livelihood strategies to repay loans, including taking on more loans to repay other loans. Referred to as "hidden delinquency" (Albee 1996) and "loan recycling" (Rahman 1999; Mpogole et al. 2012), these practices occur when groups of borrowers serve as social collateral for micro-loans. Hidden delinquency/loan recycling occurs when borrowers want to avoid the accompanying shame that comes with default. In Honduras, if someone within a micro-credit organization is unable to repay their debt, then other borrowers within the group are forced to pay it back. To avoid this, women turn to their social networks, a strategy that usually involves borrowing more money to repay loans by incurring micro-debts with friends, family members, or colleagues—people to whom they have often given credit in the past. This process of loan recycling with family and friends is labor-intensive and time-consuming, so much so that

Hayes (2017, 29) refers to it as "unpaid" labor, even though the labor of creating these social ties often ends with small amounts of much-needed cash. Borrower/creditors engage in labor- and time-consuming social interactions with others for two reasons: to foster good relationships that they can count on for future borrowing and to persuade others to repay their debts to them. Hayes states that we know very little about the hidden work of these social ties and how these social ties factor into the high rates of repayment among micro-credit borrowers.

To understand the role credit/debt plays in creating and remaking social boundaries, Peebles (2010, 230) notes that "such moments wherein credit/ debt becomes affixed to individuals or collectivities, and moves between them, allows us to witness the inscription of social boundaries of inclusion, exclusion, hierarchy, and quality." Hayes' ethnography of loan recycling in Honduras can be used to point out an important fact of life for residents living in the Callejón and La Cienaga: because unknown and temporarily unemployed shoppers are only afforded in-store credit in colmados when others vouch for them—allowing others to put their purchases on their own debt column in fiao notebooks—borrowers are often creditors. As such, borrower/ creditors must keep track of not only their own debts, but of who they vouch for and how much others owe them.

Another aspect of borrower/creditor exchanges is the hidden labor that is part of collecting debt repayment. When I have presented my research in different venues, such as at conferences or invited lectures, I often get questions about whether or not conflict or violence breaks out in the Callejón and La Cienaga because of unpaid debts in colmados. For example, after one of my presentations, a colleague's question alluded to organized crime when he asked, "What's the process of getting people to pay their debts? Are there hitmen who go around calling on people to pay up their debts?" Although Karim (2011) found an "economy of shame" that resulted in violence against defaulters in micro-credit organizations in Bangladesh, I explain to people who pose questions like this about colmado debt repayment that, to the contrary, area shopkeepers tolerate most customers' level of debt and report what they consider to be high debt repayment, as Hayes found with borrowers of micro-credit debt in Honduras. In fact, while colmaderos typically account for approximately one-third debt repayment in any given pay period, all colmaderos reported that meeting this goal maintains financial solvency in their shops. High debt repayment in Cabarete colmados is interwoven into the fabric of the social safety net of fiao and is a result of the hidden labor in which people engage to ensure that they can provision their households.

Most creditors discussed the "hard work" involved with the hidden labor of making sure people repay their debts—another sign that exemplifies and justifies their designation as gente responsable, part of the hard work of the emergent morality of fiao discussed in chapter 3. Whether the creditor is a shopkeeper or a person who vouches for another, collecting debt payment is critical to the moral economy of fiao in Cabarete. It is a laborious task that usually involves several encounters between borrower and creditor to achieve successful debt repayment. But this labor more often than not ends in debt repayment because the consequences of not paying the debt—being regarded as not responsible and therefore ineligible for fiao—are too costly. For example, Charo, a forty-two-year-old Dominican single mother of three children in La Cienaga, discussed the hard work involved with collecting what is owed to her from several people in the community. "I vouched for three people in September at Rozalín's colmado because they all moved here from [a community outside of the Dominican city of Santiago], and I spent three months going to their house to see when they would pay it back," she reported. In all, these three borrowers owed Charo RD400 (approximately US$9.30), an amount that was difficult to repay with her income as a housecleaner in two area small hotels. Charo admits that she vouched for these shoppers because they had come to the area with a promise of steady jobs: one borrower was hired at a local construction firm where his cousin was working, one borrower was seeking out jobs as a hairstylist at local salons, and another borrower was applying at area restaurants as a cook. Charo recognized the potential for future borrower/creditor exchanges with these new residents, two who were Dominican and the third was Dominico-Haitian.

Charo reported making ten different visits to the homes of these three borrowers over the course of three months. Sometimes, her arrival was met with an invitation to eat a small snack, usually a mango or a couple of pieces of fried breadfruit, and a partial repayment of what was owed to her. "I never am repaid in full in a single visit," she told me. In one of these visits, she was given 80 pesos from a borrower who owed her 120 pesos; Charo exclaimed that this high repayment rate (two-thirds of total amount owed) was rare, but she welcomed it. "That [getting 80 pesos in one visit] saved me that week because I needed to pay my own debt at Pepe's colmado," Charo said. Typically, she counts on receiving about one-third of what she is owed in any individual visit—the reward for the "hard work" in which she engages of becoming gente responsable and extending credit to others.

Based upon interviews with residents in both the Callejón and La Cienaga, Charo's experiences with borrowers' debt repayment are characteristic of other creditors in two very important ways. People who vouch for others in colmados engage in hard work, making multiple visits to borrowers' homes for repayment. In Cabarete, the person who extends credit through vouching for others is the person who engages in the hard work of collecting debt repayment. Since both men and women vouch for others, then both men and women make visits to borrowers' homes to collect. But Charo's experiences also emphasize another important characteristic of borrower/ creditor exchanges: Dominicans and Haitians are vouching for each other, which, all things considered, includes subsequent intercultural interactions to collect debt repayment. The next section further explicates these intercultural borrower/creditor exchanges among shopkeepers and customers.

BORROWER/CREDITORS, VOUCHING FOR OTHERS, AND HAITIAN-DOMINICAN RELATIONS

Throughout my fieldwork, I observed forty-two instances of people vouching for and extending credit to others so that they could make a purchase, which is an average of a little over 1.5 instances per quincenal, the typical fifteen-day pay period in the Dominican Republic. My observations of borrower/creditor exchanges took place in eleven out of the twelve colmados where I conducted participant observation. Overall, a little over half of the borrower/creditor relations were between Dominicans and Haitians (n = 22), while a little under half were between people of the same heritage (n = 20). Eight of these same-heritage borrower/creditor instances occurred between Dominicans, whereby the creditor and borrower were Dominican. In twelve cases, both borrower and creditor were Haitians. In another sixteen cases, Dominicans vouched for Haitians, and in the last six instances, Haitians vouched for Dominicans. The vast majority of these occurrences took place in person (n = 38), while just four of these instances were carried out over the phone between the creditor and the shopkeeper. In all of the fiao exchanges that I witnessed, both in person and over the phone, I was able to verify the heritage of both borrower and creditor because I had prior knowledge of the person or because I asked the people involved.

A typical borrower/creditor exchange occurred in Junior's colmado on a day like all others in the Callejón. All parties involved were Dominican. Junior's wife, Micayla, was working behind the counter when Luisa requested in-store credit to make her purchases. Luisa's oldest son was the unfortunate victim of a motorcycle accident in the previous month, and news of the accident had spread throughout the neighborhood. Paying for her son's medical bills, including treatments for a broken leg and ribs, along with the loss of his income to pay household expenses, signified to others that she may not have the ability to repay any debts. She had a page in the fiao notebook at two colmados, one of them was Junior's, but Luisa knew that her son's accident might affect any shopkeeper's assessment of her ability to be responsible, and that day, it did: Micayla's response to Luisa's request for in-store credit was answered with a request to guarantee her debt repayment, meaning that Luisa had to get someone to vouch for her. Luisa called Amelia from her cell phone, and Amelia, serendipitously in the Callejón at the time, stopped by Junior's to vouch for Luisa's purchases. Micayla put Luisa's purchases on Amelia's in-store credit page in her fiao notebook. After Luisa and Amelia left the shop, I asked Micayla about her request of Luisa: Hadn't Luisa proven herself responsible to Micayla, evidenced by her page in the fiao notebook? Why had Micayla asked for someone to vouch for Luisa in this instance? Micayla's response was telling:

> Yes, Cristina, usually Luisa is responsible, and I typically don't have to ask her to guarantee her purchase. But it's October [one of the slowest months of the year in the tourism industry], and that means we don't have a lot of income. I need to make sure she repays her debts. And Amelia is her very good friend and neighbor—having her vouch for Luisa is good. [CH: In what sense?] Amelia will help her pay for these purchases, and I will be able to repay my own bills.

While I witnessed forty-two borrower/creditor exchanges, these were not all of the borrower/creditor exchanges that took place during my fieldwork. Many people made me aware of their borrower/creditor interactions after the fact. Researching borrower/creditor relationships is difficult in the Callejón and La Cienaga for two reasons. First, it is impossible to distinguish just by reading the fiao notebooks whether or not someone vouched for another for any purchase. When someone vouches for a person, it is not recorded as such in the fiao notebook. Only the amount of the purchase is listed, not if the exchange was made by someone who extended credit to someone else for the purchase. Therefore, if I did not observe the borrower/creditor exchange, my only recourse was to inquire and rely on people's recall of their prior interactions. Second, most people are not forthcoming with information about the specifics for whom they vouch because of the inherent risk involved. If a borrower finds out that a creditor failed to vouch for them in a specific instance, but did so for another borrower, this could be interpreted as a slight and might create conflict. Or conversely, if people find out that a creditor is someone they know, the creditor might become overwhelmed with requests to vouch for potential borrowers in a particular colmado, a very risky prospect for the creditor if the borrowers might not be able to pay off debts. Therefore, it would have jeopardized my rapport in the community if I had used specific ethnographic methods to get these data, such as daily journals from colmaderos who could have recorded these exchanges or social network analysis which would require me to routinely survey residents for a list of people for whom they had vouched. Instead, I inquired about borrower/creditor exchanges with ten interviewees with whom I had extensive interaction, those who were confident that I wouldn't share this information with anyone else or exploit it in any way. None of the forty-two borrower/creditor direct observations I made in colmados included interactions with these interviewees. These interviewees varied in age, gender, and heritage. Six were women and four were men; eight were under forty years old and the other two were in their fifties, and five were Dominican and five were Haitian or of Haitian descent. All ten interviewees—no matter their heritage—reported that they had made borrower/creditor exchanges with both Dominicans and Haitians.

For example, Oscar, a forty-one-year-old Dominican who has lived in La Cienaga for twelve years, regularly buys food on credit in three colmados: Ana's, Jonás', and Pepe's, the same Pepe from the story at the beginning of this chapter. Like most residents in the Callejón and La Cienaga, Oscar engages in multiple livelihood strategies in Cabarete. He speaks three languages to varying degrees—Spanish, German, and English—which he uses in his positions as a local tour guide and as a part-time after-school teacher in a local NGO. Additionally, every couple of months Oscar fills in as a motoconcho driver for his cousin, and they split the profits Oscar makes for the days he works. Oscar's jobs as a tour guide, teacher, and motoconchista expose him not only to many tourists but also to local residents who work in the tourism industry. Using these three income-generating strategies, Oscar is quite well-known as gente responsable and is almost never denied fiao in colmados. And he has earned this distinction despite the gaps in his income during the ebbs and flows of the tourist economy. When I ask him if he ever shops using fiao in other colmados, he says no, he doesn't have to: "I don't need to shop elsewhere because they [Ana, Jonás, and Pepe] know I'm responsible, so they give me fiao" replies Oscar.

Over the course of the twelve years that Oscar has lived in Cabarete, he has vouched for more than twenty people throughout the Callejón and La Cienaga in Ana's, Jonás', and Pepe's colmados. He has learned to successfully provision his household by strategically and exclusively shopping at these three colmados, and when asked, vouching for new shoppers from different spheres of his life for Ana, Jonás, and Pepe. Each of these shopkeepers is of a different heritage: Ana is Haitian, Jonás is Dominico-Haitian, and Pepe is Dominican. Oscar has vouched for shoppers who have become important gente responsable at each of these colmados. When I inquired about the criteria he uses for deciding when and with whom to extend credit, he explained:

Cristina, this can be a mess if I don't do it right. For example, if I say yes to someone who I know is not working, or I know has a hard time keeping a job, then not only does the shopkeeper suffer, but I'm going to suffer too, you know? I may have 3 different jobs, but I need people to pay me back if I help them out. When there are no tourists, I don't work for my cousin, I barely have 2 jobs then. I have to say yes to the right people. Sometimes, the right people might be someone I know is a hard worker, who has a job, but they just moved to the neighborhood and they don't make much money. [CH: Like what?] You know, they moved here from Haiti and they have family back home, and he works helping out a friend who landscapes, but he doesn't have steady work. [CH: Like who?] Yes, this is Josué. I vouched for him when he first came to Cabarete [in 2014] at Pepe's colmado . . . Pepe didn't want to do it [give him fiao], but Pepe trusted me. Now, Josué has his own page in Pepe's notebook. Josué works hard, both to get jobs but also to repay his debt . . . to me and to colmaderos. He is like my *primo hermano* [first cousin] . . . he is like family. Besides, Josué has lent me money when I've needed it, too. One day, I needed gas for the motorcycle taxi and I wouldn't have been able to work that day if Josué didn't lend me cash for it.

Oscar makes it clear that he trusts Josué as he would a close family member, like a first cousin (the child of his parents' siblings), explaining that this fictive kinship is based in part on the consistent reciprocal exchanges in which they have engaged over the years. Oscar's vouching for Josué led to Pepe trusting him well enough to give Josué his own fiao notebook page. In fact, Josué is one of the Haitians to whom Pepe regularly gives in-store credit—even though he claims that "all Haitians are thieves" and that "he can't trust them."

Colmaderos often made reference to the fact that their religious beliefs and moral compass inspire them to extend fiao because they themselves were but one hardship, one unpaid debt, one catastrophe away from needing assistance. Sintia, another interviewee, points out the importance of the shopkeeper's role as gatekeepers to fiao. She is a thirty-five-year-old Dominican woman who has made borrower/creditor exchanges in two different colmados—one in the Callejón and another in La Cienaga. When I asked her about these exchanges, she confirmed that she has vouched for "many" different people and proceeded to recount stories using the names of eight people, including a recent exchange she made in Rosalín's colmado for Daniel, a Haitian migrant who had been living in Cabarete for about a year before he started dating Sintia (and discussed in my fieldnotes at the beginning of chapter 3). Because Rosalín considers Sintia gente responsable, she took a chance on Daniel by allowing him to make purchases and put these charges on Sintia's tab. When I asked how many times Rosalín allowed this, Sintia states,

I don't know, I think 5 times? It took a little while because Rosalín didn't know Daniel so well . . . he used to live in Pista Motocross [another neighborhood about 8 km away from La Cienaga]. [CH: What took a while?] Well, Rosalín didn't know if she could consider him responsible. But once she saw that I paid my debt to her, and Daniel paid me what he owed so that I could pay my debt, Rosalín gave him a page in her fiao notebook. Now, he doesn't need me to help him [keep his tab]. Rosalín often tells me, "May God bless you," and tells me that fiao is a gift from God to help her eat, too. Rosalín knows that with my help, I bring to her shoppers who become gente responsable and will repay debts and with these payments, she is able to pay her own debt.

Like Sintia's relationship with Rosalín, an important characteristic of determining gente responsable accounts for the ability a creditor has to recruit borrowers who can be trusted to pay off their loans to shopkeepers. An example to illustrate this is the case of Wilman and Teresa,[1] Haitian customers who regularly shopped using fiao in Edison's colmado. Like some other Dominican colmaderos, Edison exclaimed to me one day when I was conducting participant observation in his shop, "Haitians are not good customers—they never pay their debt and I can't trust them. Haitians are all thieves . . . they never pay their debts, Cristina! Can you imagine that?" And like other conversations with shopkeepers, his words confused me because I specifically knew of at least six Haitians that Edison gives fiao to on an almost-daily basis, like Wilman.

Wilman had migrated to the Dominican Republic in 2004 after Hurricane George destroyed his former home of Fond Verrettes in southeastern Haiti, where his parents, most of his eight siblings, and their families still live. When Wilman initially entered the Dominican Republic, he worked for a few months on a sugarcane plantation near Barahona in southwestern Dominican Republic, and then moved on to work for three years as a groundskeeper in a small, family-run hotel southeast of Puerto Plata. Then in 2009, he settled into his current position as a handyman and gardener at a couple of apartment complexes in Cabarete. When I first met Wilman's wife, Teresa, she had only been living with Wilman in the Dominican Republic for four months, having migrated from Haiti first to the Dominican city of Moca to receive medical attention for tumors found in her uterus. She moved to the Callejón to live with her husband and recover from surgery. Throughout my research, Wilman and Teresa would often, but not exclusively, shop at Edison's colmado because it was 100 meters away from their home. Sometimes, Wilman and Teresa would invite me to their home for a mid-day meal, which consisted of rice, bean sauce, meat, and a small salad with home-made dressing. Since Teresa was recovering from surgery, I would often arrive early to help her shop and cook, which consisted of at least one visit, sometimes more, to Edison's colmado. Each visit with her meant that I had full knowledge of how much Teresa and Wilman owed Edison. Wilman and Teresa's debts always totaled more than the amount they spent when I was present, proving that Edison consistently offered them fiao even when I wasn't present during the transaction.

While Wilman and Teresa benefited from fiao in Edison's colmado, Wilman's role in these balanced reciprocal exchanges was equally important to Edison: Wilman not only regularly repaid his debt, facilitated by the fact that he was well respected as a hardworking and reliable handyman in his places of employment, but he also consistently vouched for other Haitians in the community who asked Edison for in-store credit. And these borrowers consistently repaid their debts to both Wilman and Edison. Edison's colmado was financially better off with Wilman as a trusted customer because he brought in more customers who became gente responsable. This, in turn, helped Edison repay his own debt to distributors.

During my research, I typically asked Haitians and Dominicans about their relationships with the Other, especially if others had vouched for them in the past or if anyone had neglected to repay debts owed to them. In Wilman's case, he could recall only one instance when someone he had vouched for, a Dominican, left town before repaying his debt. I inquired as to whether or not that affected any subsequent decisions he made to vouch for Dominicans. Wilman's response was an adamant, "no," and he recounted six subsequent instances in which he vouched for Dominican shoppers who had just moved to the area and needed references to establish themselves as gente responsable.

GENDER AND BORROWER/CREDITOR EXCHANGES

When it comes to fiao exchanges, gender has some effect on people's decisions to allow a customer to buy food on credit or to vouch for them in colmados. Unlike other studies of shopping in corner stores (e.g., Deustch 2001), women are not the only shoppers in colmados in the Callejón and La Cienaga nor are men the only shopkeepers. As discussed in chapter 2, women are most likely to be found shopping in colmados in the morning to buy food needed to make the midday meal, and sometimes, if women were too busy cooking or working in other capacities, they send their children to colmados in their stead. More often than not, men typically shop on their way home from work at midday or after work in the evening. Their wives regularly ask men to stop at a local colmado before they return home from work to buy something that could be cooked by their wives that day or the next morning. Men often select to shop at a colmado that transitions into a colmadón in the evening so they can listen to music, drink beer or rum, and converse with friends.

Yet while both men and women shop in colmados, they receive fiao as a household, not as individuals. For example, Teresa earned the reputation for being gente responsable like her husband, not only in Edison's shop but also in other colmados. While Wilman had lived in Cabarete since 2009, Teresa's more recent arrival in 2014 meant that she had a much less comprehensive history of using fiao than her husband did. Since her arrival in the Callejón, Teresa had never been denied fiao in any colmados where she requested it. But she knows to only ask to make purchases on a tab in the colmados where

her husband has a page in the fiao notebook. This was common practice in
Cabarete: when men, women, and children made purchases using fiao, it was
documented under their household name, usually using the first and last name
of the adult male in the household. Therefore, fiao as a system is more patriar-
chal, insomuch as household debt is documented under men's names. But in
the absence of an adult male, a woman's name is used to represent the household, and all household debts incurred would then be listed under her name.

Gender is invoked frequently, but not exclusively, when it comes to vouching for someone in colmados. Habitually, women make requests of other
women to vouch for them to make them eligible for fiao in corner stores, and
men do the same for men. Less frequently, women vouch for men and vice
versa, as in the case of Sintia vouching for Daniel in Rozalín's colmado in the
fieldnotes story that began chapter 3. For the forty-two observations of bor-
rower/creditor exchanges in all of the colmados where these exchanges were
made, figure 4.1 lays out the intersections of creditors' gender and heritage.
Women served as creditors in two-thirds of the total exchanges made (28/42)
and women served as creditors twice as many times as men did (twenty-eight
women creditors and fourteen men). This is not all that surprising because it
is almost equal to the percentage of women who shop in colmados throughout
each day (about 64%, explained in chapter 2). Of the twenty-two total intercultural exchanges, Dominican women served as creditors for Haitians ten
out of sixteen times, while Haitian women and men equally served as creditors for Dominicans (three out of six times, respectively). Of the twenty intracultural exchanges, Dominican women served as creditors for Dominicans
and Haitian women served as creditors for Haitians 75% of the time.

Gender also has an impact on shopkeepers' decision-making about
when and how to extend different types of fiao to their customers. In
Teresa's case, she benefited from her husband Wilman's responsible past

Table 4.1   Observed Intercultural and Intracultural Borrower/Creditor Exchanges, by Gender and Heritage of Creditor

Intercultural Borrower/Creditor Exchanges (n = 22)				Intracultural Borrower/Creditor Exchanges (n = 20)			
Gender of creditor	Men	Women	Total	Gender of creditor	Men	Women	Total
Dominican vouched for Haitian	6	10	16	Dominican vouched for Dominican	2	6	8
Haitian vouched for Dominican	3	3	6	Haitian vouched for Haitian	3	9	12
Total	9	13	22	Total	5	15	20

Figure 4.1   A Struggling Colmado. Photo taken by the author.

behavior. Wilman's distinction as gente responsable assuaged colmaderos, who allowed Teresa, by extension, to make purchases using in-store credit. But sometimes women were limited in accessing fiao because of the men in their lives. When a household reaches their maximum limit of in-store credit, other members of the household may be denied in-store credit, especially if a man uses fiao to make what is perceived to be a morally dubious charge, such as drinking rum or beer at colmadones. This was discussed in chapter 3, when Aryceli, the more financially secure resident of the Callejón who vilified fiao, informed me that Abril suffered and had to work harder to earn more money to pay off the debts incurred when her husband, Oscar, used in-store credit in colmadones.

Furthermore, it is common knowledge that female shopkeepers, more often than male shopkeepers, are those who are called upon to make gifts to shoppers in dire need. While my sample of women shopkeepers is very small (only five colmados were owned or partially owned by women in the Callejón and La Cienaga), it is interesting to note that most shoppers reported that they would seek out women working in colmados, either as shopkeepers or ayudantes, when they needed a gift, the second type of fiao in which a shopper requests to purchase something using in-store credit with the understanding that the debt would most likely not be repaid. This could be read as an example of what Sanabria (2007) refers to as *marianismo* or the hegemonic gender ideology for women in Latin America that prescribes the virtues of selflessness and submissiveness for women. Female shopkeepers are expected to be more compassionate by sacrificing or behaving in more selfless ways by acquiescing to requests for gifts. Likewise, this expectation of "virtuous womanhood" is found elsewhere in the Caribbean. Garth (2020) indicates that women in Cuba are burdened with behaving in certain virtuous ways in their pursuit and acquisition of "a decent meal." In colmados in Cabarete, a virtuous womanhood is signified by a feminist ethics of care (i.e., Gilligan and Noddings 2009) or norms which "direct our attention to the need for responsiveness in relationships (paying attention, listening, responding) and to the costs of losing connection with oneself or with others" (Gilligan 2011). In fact, it could be argued that this expectation of virtuous womanhood using a feminist ethics of care is what drives many types of hidden labor, whether it might be providing shoppers with gifts in colmados in my own research or attempting to acquire informal loans from friends and family to repay formal debts to microfinance organizations, as did women in Hayes' case study in Honduras (2017).

Like Teresa indicated in the fieldnotes story at the beginning of the introduction, shoppers frequently told me that women are more apt to show compassion for them in their dire need. But this kind of sacrifice and compassion can lead to financial ruin. With only a handful of female shopkeepers in these neighborhoods, it is uncommon for shopkeepers to get requests for gifts. However, it is also important to keep in mind that shopkeepers, no matter their gender, are not able to acquiesce to all requests for gifts of fiao. If they did, their colmados would go bankrupt.

Although borrower/creditor exchanges are ubiquitous in the Callejón and La Cienaga, debt repayment is not always achieved. There are other examples in which borrower/creditors are not repaid, like the Dominican borrower who skipped town after Wilman vouched for him, and this has serious consequences for the economy in these neighborhoods. Sometimes, extending in-store credit to others can result in failed relationships between creditors and borrowers who fail to repay, as well as financial ruin for colmados. And as I discuss in the next section, with so few colmados owned and staffed by women in Cabarete, it is not coincidental that two out of the three most financially insolvent colmados in the area belong to women.

THE FAILURE OF FIAO AND
STRUGGLING COLMADOS

One of the most prominent characteristic features of struggling colmados was the lack of borrower/creditor exchanges made. Out of the twelve different colmados in which I engaged in participant observation, three of them were considered failing, meaning that their shop often could not afford to stock their shelves. It is not difficult to spot a failing colmado: they are often what people call "empty" (*vacío*, in Spanish). Empty refers to not only a slim selection of inventory, but it also denotes a lack of customers in the shop, or at the very least, a lack of customers who buy from a colmado. In the three colmados considered failing in which I worked, customers would often enter only to ask if a certain product was available, sometimes to be told of its absence by the shopkeeper, which would prompt the customer to abruptly take leave to search for what they needed in another colmado. All failing colmados were owned by Haitians or Dominico-Haitians: Ana, Jonás, and Anouz. Situated in both the Callejón and La Cienaga, the location of these colmados had nothing to do with their financial insolvency. According to all three shopkeepers, overextending in-store credit resulted in the spiral of debt that prevented them from consistently staying in business. Shopkeeping in failing colmados is typified by giving credit as if everyone were gente responsable; in other words, they seldom require people to vouch for each other and therefore have fewer borrower/creditor exchanges to mitigate the risk of extending credit to customers, particularly those customers who have fallen on hard times or are unknown.

Jonás' colmado in La Cienaga was the most struggling shop in which I worked. At times, I would arrive at his shop to a locked door and shuttered windows, even in the middle of the day. He closed his doors periodically, "sometimes once or twice a month for a couple of days," he reported, when his shop was empty so that he could work a few extra hours as an on-again-off-again clerk in a tourist shop in downtown Cabarete. His income from the tourist shop allowed him to repay his own debts to distributors, which in turn resulted in more inventory for his shop. Despite these efforts, he never seemed to secure enough revenue to cease his periodic shop closures. However paradoxical it may seem, shutting his doors led to more fiao, not less, to build a bigger base of customers who shopped at his store. Jonás admitted that this strategy often backfired on him, especially when he allowed people to purchase using in-store credit when they had previously had problems repaying their debts to Jonás. He rarely denies someone fiao, "[I only deny fiao to those] who have walked away from their debts to me before, usually many times," he explains.

While the other nine colmaderos with whom I worked reported that people typically repaid 30% of their debts every quincenal, shopkeepers in the three failing colmados were known to take in a smaller proportion of debt repayment within any given pay period. For example, Jonás, the shopkeeper with the most failing colmado in my research sample, reported that debt repayment in his colmado was approximately 10% each pay period. I confirmed this with a review of his fiao notebook: when customers made debt repayments, indicated by a scratched-out sum with the leftover debt recorded next to it, I found that almost every customer repaid approximately only 10% of their debts owed to Jonás in any given pay period. "This really isn't enough to keep getting by," he explained to me.

> I can't pay my own bills, which makes me give more in-store credit. Do you see? I have just as many pages in my notebook as a big store like Pepe does. But people don't pay enough to me to keep my shop going. I give fiao to people who don't get in-store credit at other colmados. I'm their last stop. [CH: How does this affect your store?] Well, I'm not able to buy inventory, that's for sure. Don't you see my bare shelves and bins? Customers come to my shop, but I don't have much to offer. That's why I have to close my shop every once in a while, that and I have to work [at my other job] so that my kids can eat. Being a shopkeeper doesn't allow me to get by.

More often than not, shopkeepers in struggling colmados, like Jonás, allowed customers to purchase using in-store credit without someone to vouch for them. There were fewer borrower/creditor relationships mani-fested in two out of the three struggling colmados than there were at the other colmados in which I worked. In fact, during my fieldwork, I never once observed a borrower/creditor exchange in Jonás' colmado—the only colmado in which I failed to witness this type of exchange. When I inquired about bor-rower/creditor exchanges in his colmado, Jonás indeed told me that he rarely requested that a customer find someone to vouch for them. "I have asked only a couple of people to find someone to vouch for them, but only a couple of times within the last year," he revealed when I asked him. "Most of the time, customers don't have anyone to vouch for them, and I know that's why they come to my store." Jonás' statement points out that his customers are typically those who have exhausted their social ties because they have been unable to repay their debts to those who have vouched for them in the past.

Jonás' notebook included customers who had pages in fiao notebooks in other colmados. What was notable was that while these customers only paid 10% of their debts at Jonás' colmado, these same customers paid more of their debts at other colmados, including other struggling colmados, such as Ana's, which was not as far into financial ruin as Jonás' shop. Her notebook showed that customers repaid about 20% of their debts in any given pay period. Ana is the Haitian shopkeeper who, as discussed in chapter 2, trav-els to Haiti every so often and delivers Haitian products to customers in the Callejón and La Cienaga. She charges 50 pesos (approximately US$1.20) for this service, which is the same delivery charge customers pay motoconcho drivers to make home deliveries from local colmados. Even with this added charge, customers who pay on a tab repay more of their debts to Ana each month than they do to Jonás. Ana divulged that without at least a 20% debt repayment, she would not be able to regularly travel to Haiti to purchase desired products for customers in the Callejón and La Cienaga. Ana explains:

> I have to pay for my bus fare and my food to get there, you know? If I have a customer who fails to pay their debts, then I refuse to purchase Haitian products for them. Well, sometimes I do . . . I'm in Haiti anyway to buy stuff for other people, so why not make the purchase for them, too? But I usually don't require people to find someone to vouch for them. Frankly, if I tell customers that I won't buy Haitian products for them if they fail to repay, they pay enough of their debts. [CH: But you told me it's hard for you to buy inventory. Do you think people pay enough of their debts for your colmado to survive?] I struggle, but it's not impossible. I get by.

But Haitians are not Ana's only customers. Ana's colmado in the Callejón attracts Dominican customers as well. Interestingly, out of the six observations I made of Haitians vouching for Dominicans during my fieldwork, three of them were in Ana's colmado. Ana explained that she has two Haitian customers who have vouched for Dominican customers in Ana's colmado: Yani, who works for a construction company, and Simon, who works for the ProCab neighborhood as a streetcleaner. Ana explains to me that her colmado is better off because of the customers for whom Yani and Simon vouch. "Yani and Simon are both responsible people, so when they vouch for customers, I know that I'll be paid." Because she does a lot of her business with Haitians who request purchases made on her travels to Haiti, Ana admits that she is unfamiliar with a lot of Dominicans in the neighborhood, and Yani and Simon are helpful in vouching for Dominican shoppers. There have been two customers in the recent past who Yani and Simon vouched for but who moved away from Cabarete before they repaid their debt, leaving Yani and Simon to repay these debts to Ana. "Thank God these debts weren't too costly, just about 100 pesos each [US$2.33] if I'm not mistaken, so I've allowed Yani and Simon to pay them gradually to me," recounted Ana. "Do experiences like these make you pause before giving in-store credit to Dominicans?" I asked Ana. "Well no," she replied. "Without Dominicans, my colmado would be in ruin. More Dominicans repay their debts than not."

For reasons explained in chapter 2, being a shopkeeper is a desirable profession but is seldom a route to the middle class. All parties involved with fiao—shopkeepers and customers—are of the same social class: working class and/or poor. But shopkeepers of failing colmados emphasized their vulnerability and indicated that running a colmado feels a lot like working within the ebb and flow of the local tourist economy, jobs held by most of

their customers. For example, in a conversation I had with her in her struggling colmado, Anouz told me:

> You know . . . sometimes I don't have much in my store to sell, and customers
> leave my store unhappy and dissatisfied. This happens when I can't pay my
> distributors. [CH: Because you paid on a tab?] Yes, I can't pay my own tab
> when others [customers] don't pay off enough of their debts. [Before I was a
> shopkeeper] I used to work every day as a masseuse . . . walking the beaches for
> tourists who I would massage for a fee. Sometimes I would find work, and other
> times there would be no work. [Chuckles] I guess I still feel like that. Being a
> shopkeeper still gives me no security. I thought that being a shopkeeper might
> keep me from having to ask others to borrow money . . . I find that I do just that
> all the time to keep my shop afloat.

Anouz sometimes requires customers to solicit someone to vouch for them.
While this has prevented customers from walking away from their debts, it
also has resulted in people repaying only about 15% of their debt in any given
pay period. Anouz encourages borrower/creditor relationships for new customers who are unknown to her, but she does not require someone to vouch
for a customer who is unemployed at the time of the purchase. "I have to be
loyal to customers who I know, whether working or not, so that they continue
to come shop at my store. Only then will they be loyal to me."

THE FAILURE OF FIAO AND FOOD-
SHARING AMONG RESIDENTS

Although failing colmados are often viewed as a venue of last resort for
customers who experience difficulty attaining fiao, even these colmados
deny some customers the opportunity of purchasing on credit. Intriguingly,
while colmados' doors are often closed to customers who are unable to find a
way to become gente responsable, people frequently open the doors of their
homes to others in times of need. Residents in the Callejón and La Cienaga
often have people stop by during the midday meal or in the evening to see
if they will be invited to sit down to eat. People sometimes have to travel
widely in the neighborhood or have to go to more than one house to succeed
in garnering an invitation to share a meal. At times, instead of a meal, people
might succeed in attaining a gift from someone's home, such as an avocado,
mango, or some cooked rice. None of these gifts are considered meals in and
of themselves but are viewed as a helpful exchange by both the giver and the
receiver because of the promise—usually unspoken—of future exchanges in
times of need.

During my fieldwork, I inquired about food- and meal-sharing specifically during times of need, when residents were most inclined to be denied fiao in area colmados. Out of forty interviewees who indicated that they shared food and meals when they were denied fiao, thirty-nine of them reported that they did so with non-household members for at least one meal a week. Twenty-five of them relayed that they shared food and meals with others at least three times a week. And twelve respondents indicated that they shared food and meals with others outside of their households every day of the week. All respondents told me that they had to travel more to find a shared meal in the evening, when they sometimes would have to travel to up to four homes to do so. For those people who typically shared meals at midday, they could count on being invited to share a meal after travelling to only one or two homes. Only one interviewee reported seldom sharing any of his meals. "I don't ask anyone else for food or meals when I can't get fiao in colmados. I usually just go without, usually I eat just a small mid-day meal and then eat the next morning. Well, sometimes I bring a coconut or mango to a friend and they might feed me, but this isn't every week . . . maybe once a month," Isayis explained.

Meal-sharing occurs not only when tourism slows, but also in times of individual crises. For example, when Luisa's son was injured in a car accident, Luisa found it difficult to buy food on credit in corner stores. Amelia, her friend and neighbor, was not always available to vouch for her, as she did in Junior's colmado discussed in the beginning of this chapter. But Luisa's house was a well-known stop for many as they travelled to find someone to share a meal during times of need. The fieldnotes story shared at the beginning of chapter 3, with Luisa, Amelia, Samuel, and Daniel, is a story of meal-sharing in this way: Samuel and Daniel had heard that Luisa, Amelia, and I were making sancocho over an open fire and knew that Luisa would not turn them away. While Luisa's son was recovering from his car accident, she and her youngest son, a ten-year-old boy, shared meals every night for a week at Samuel and Aurelys' house, located right up the street from Luisa's house in Pista Motocross. Aurelys generously fried salami and eggs for herself, Samuel, Luisa, and her young son for a light meal. "I don't know what I would have done without Samuel and Aurelys," exclaimed Luisa when I asked her about her taking meals with them. "Yes, I have fed them both many times, but never for a whole week, like I ate with them."

Esther, a thirty-five-year-old Haitian hairstylist, routinely ate almost every night of the week with Teresa and Wilman in the Callejón. A newcomer to Cabarete, Esther had moved to the community in 2013 to attain medical care in nearby Sosúa to treat endometriosis and resultant chronic pain. Esther grew up in Portoprens, the capital of Haiti, where she attended college to become a kindergarten teacher, and after graduation taught for three years in a private elementary school one hour north of the city. Esther quit teaching after working for seven months with no pay, and the school closed its doors soon thereafter. Serendipitously, Esther's friend invited her to work for a cruise line whose operations centered in the Bahamas, so Esther moved to the Bahamas and worked on the ship for five years. It was during this time that the symptoms of her endometriosis appeared and gradually worsened to the point where she was forced to quit her job. She moved to Cabarete because her cousin had been living there and told Esther that she would care for her during her treatment.

Esther's treatment in Sosúa included a hysterectomy, which precluded the possibility of having her own children and starting a family. Esther remained in Cabarete living with her cousin even after she recovered from her surgery. "I don't think of myself as a religious person," she told me, but she attended the local Haitian church with her cousin and got a job there as the girls' dance troupe director. While the job was a volunteer position, at times she was invited to meals with different members of the church and their families. But Esther told me the true reason she accepted the position as the dance troupe director was because "it's a way to show people in the community that I really was trained as a teacher." She used her meager savings to take a hair-styling class in a technical school in Sosúa. But since she was undocumented, she realized that she would never be issued the requisite state work license, so she ceased her formal studies to save money. When I met her, she had been working without papers for three years braiding hair in a tourist shop near the Cabarete beaches. This income distinguished her as gente responsable most of the time, and she garnered pages in fiao notebooks in two colmados in the Callejón, one of which was Jonás' struggling colmado. But Esther was the first hairstylist to be laid off when tourism decreased, and it was then that she was denied fiao.

"Teresa and Wilman save me," Esther made clear to me one day while a number of us were eating at Teresa and Wilman's house on a Sunday afternoon.

> I eat at Teresa's at night, and I will sometimes bring an avocado, an onion, or some cheese for her to fry up, if I have money. But if I don't have money, and I can't buy at Jonás' colmado [because she is denied fiao], Teresa always invites me to come eat with her and Wilman, even at mid-day. Actually, it was through Wilman vouching for me that I earned a page in fiao notebooks, first with Jonás and then with Rozalín. Sometimes, Teresa and Wilman don't have enough food to go around, so I have to look for a meal in other places, like Anouz's down the street, or with Michelín.

Esther's words highlight a relevant issue with meal-sharing: people are some-times turned away not because they are not welcome, but because people are suffering from their own lack and do not have anything to give. Refusing to meal-share seldom leads to hard feelings or discontent. In fact, I found people returning again and again to people who had previously turned them away. "My friendship with Teresa and Wilman . . . I'm still friends with them even if I can't eat with them. They give to me when they have it, and sometimes they are not able to."

Two residents relayed a unique strategy of urban-rural exchanges in which they participated to help them get by during times of need. About once a month, Nino and Genesis in the Callejón exchanged food raised by their friends who lived in Loma, a rural community located near the foothills of the Cordillera Septentrional about forty-five minutes away. Nino and Genesis would invite these friends to spend a night or two at their house when they came to the Callejón to sell their produce and homemade stewed beans to area colmados. "They sometimes bring us a chicken when they come stay with us," Genesis told me. "But most of the time they bring us yucca or stewed beans or fruit or plantains." I asked them if they count on these exchanges as part of their normal budgeting, or did they consider these exchanges atypical and inconsistent. "Oh no, we would not eat without these visits. They come regularly and we rely on them," replied Nino.

While intercultural borrower/creditor exchanges were common (at least as common as, or a little more so than, intracultural borrower/creditor exchanges), it was less common for me to encounter intercultural food-sharing, such as the case of Luisa and her son (Dominicans) eating with Samuel (Haitian) and Aurelys (Dominican). Almost all residents, both Dominicans and Haitians, reported that they had developed borrower/creditor relationships between people of the other heritage, but when I inquired about food-sharing with interviewees, they responded that they shared food less interculturally than they vouched. Dominicans consistently told me that they seldom shared meals and/or food with Haitians, and Haitians said about the same regarding Dominicans. "It does happen," said Belkis, referring to intercultural Dominican and Haitian food-sharing practices,

> but it is less common. [I am Dominican], and I don't usually ask for Haitians to provide a meal for me, but I have asked Michelín, my [Haitian] neighbor, to vouch for me in colmados . . . like at Ana's store. You know, Michelín works as a maid [in a local hotel], so that is helpful [to me] when she has an income, when she has work.

When I posed the question as to why people would be more apt to vouch for someone else's debt than they were to invite them to a meal, some respondents indicated that this was not the right question. Instead, they told me that making a request of someone as a creditor and to share a meal might provoke discomfort and be viewed as an informal breach of contract, or a sort of unreciprocated appeal; in other words, they might be asking too much of people. When I asked him about the absence of intercultural meal-sharing, Gustavo paused for a moment, looked away from me to face the group of children playing a baseball game in the street in front of his house, frowned, and thoughtfully replied:

> Frankly, Cristina, I don't really know [why I don't ask a Haitian to share a meal with me]. I think that I would invite someone into my home who I had given credit to at a colmado, but you're right . . . they just don't ask. I don't know how to answer you except to say that we are all just trying to get by . . . usually, people pay their debt because they want someone else to help them later. But maybe people are just afraid of being turned down if they ask for a meal? Maybe they are uncomfortable because they owe them money? Asking for a meal while owing them money might be too much. I don't know . . . inviting them to a meal . . . I would get to know them better I suppose. [CH: Why? Because you would converse with them?] Yes . . . but I hope I would invite them if they asked me.

CONCLUSIONS

Becoming gente responsable is a process that requires a certain amount of hidden labor of borrowers and creditors, both shoppers and shopkeepers, to provision their households and maintain their corner stores. Colmaderos and customers, borrowers and creditors are engaged in a socioeconomic system that pivots upon stakeholders' shared commonalities—their class—rather than their differences—their racial/ethnic group or heritage. Becoming gente responsable means engaging in borrower/creditor exchanges in which people are good to their word, pay off their debt, and vouch for others when they ask. These exchanges include the hard work of ensuring that debts are repaid while allowing people to cast a wide net so they can count on these people in times of need. In fact, residents engage in intercultural borrower/creditor exchanges a little more often than they engage in intracultural exchanges. Both shopkeepers and shoppers recognize the value of creditors who recruit shoppers who will prove themselves as responsable. Even when people simultaneously refer to the Other using exclusionary, derogatory, or prejudicial language, their borrowing and crediting practices are more inclusive. Dominicans and Haitians regularly vouch for each other, and debt repayment rates are considered within the range of normal except in failing colmados, where rates of debt repayment are low for all borrowers compared to debt repayment in more financially successful colmados.

Just as a little over half of colmado shoppers are women, so, too, do more women than men engage in borrower/creditor exchanges with other shoppers. Typically, women vouch for women and men vouch for men, but occasionally people transgress this norm, especially when people form new heterosexual relationships and households. Gender is invoked when shoppers are desperate and request a gift from colmaderos. Shoppers report that they seek out women who work in colmados to request gifts. But shoppers infrequently ask for gifts because there are few women who work in colmados, and it is well known that shopkeepers' financial health is maintained when they limit the number of gifts that are given.

Being a shopkeeper is a precarious job, and shopkeepers note that their lives are just as vulnerable to the area's mercurial economy as their customers. Sometimes fiao does not serve as a safety net but rather a threat. Failing colmados are characterized as empty, of both products and customers. The three most financially unstable colmados in the Callejón and La Cienaga are all owned by Haitians, and two out of three of these shopkeepers are women. Shopkeepers whose colmados are failing feel pressure to offer in-store credit to shoppers, but this strategy often results in overextending in-store credit to people who are unable to repay it or who fail to repay enough of their debt to sustain the store. When people are denied fiao, they often engage in food-sharing practices that include meal-sharing and direct food exchanges. However, food-sharing in the Callejón and La Cienaga is less intercultural than are borrower/creditor exchanges. An analysis of borrower/creditor exchanges and food-sharing practices reveals that intercultural relations between Haitians and Dominicans can be fostered in one venue while at the same time people refrain from using these intercultural relations in their networks of food-sharing. Using in-store credit to buy food in colmados in the Callejón and La Cienaga are spaces where intercultural engagement is maintained and reproduced, yet based upon both my own observations as well as people's responses to direct questioning, food-sharing practices do not yet yield the same results.

NOTE

1. Teresa is the woman in the fieldnotes featured in the introduction, the story of the first encounter I had in Cabarete with fiao.

Conclusion

"Fíame, Por Favor"—*Ties*
That Bind in Cabarete

12 March 2015

"Fíame, por favor [put it on my tab, please]," requested Emely, for the 20 pesos bag of uncooked rice, bouillon, carrots, and an eggplant she purchased at Colmado Ana to cook for the mid-day meal. I saw that Emely's page in the fiao notebook had a lengthy list of crossed-out purchases, almost running into the next page, indicating that she had had a tab at Colmado Ana for a long time. Emely and I walked out of the colmado with her purchases and made our way down Main Street in the Callejón, dodging tardy children who were running to the neighborhood elementary school. Our conversation turned to her disappointment with a slow Carnival season, which had just ended, and her anticipation of the upcoming Semana Santa, or the holy week leading up to Easter Sunday, two of the most important weeks for the tourism industry as family members from other parts of the country and international tourists vacationed in the area. Emely made a point to tell me how vital Semana Santa was to her household income, garnered from her job as a food server in a popular bar and grille along the beachfront in downtown Cabarete. When there are no diners, Emely is sent home from work, meaning that she fails to earn money that she needs to feed herself, her sister, and her sister's two young children, who rent a small one-room abode on Sixth Street in the Callejón.

"I didn't make much money during Carnival this year. Some years I do, but this year was slow," she explained to me.

"Have you been able to keep up with your tabs?" I asked her. Emely had participated extensively in my research in the Callejón. She knew well that I was inquiring because she had informed me previously that she had fallen behind on repaying one of the people who had vouched for her in Junior's colmado last month.

"Well, you know," she replied, "last month I was unable to repay Camila who had vouched for me with Micayla [Junior's wife]. I gave her [Camila] 20 pesos here, 20 pesos there, but I couldn't even repay her the 200 pesos she put on her tab for me. It worries me that Carnival was slow . . . I wonder if Semana Santa will be slow. That would be bad."

"How often are you unable to repay those who vouch for you when you endure a slow season?" I asked her.

"There are times when I don't even eat a grain of rice, times when I ask someone to vouch for me and they tell me no, times when I hide from someone who I owe money. This is true now, maybe this will continue for a little while because Semana Santa will be slow, too. But Camila is patient, thank God for her," Emely replied, referring to Camila's willingness to allow Emely to repay her bit by bit.

"Is Ana taking a risk by allowing you to purchase on your tab, even when she knows that you might not be able to repay her quickly?" I asked.

"Well, you know . . . yes, I think it is a risk, even though she knows that I will pay her gradually, but it might not be fast enough [for Ana to repay her own debt]. Thank God for Ana—she never requires me to put my purchases on someone else's tab. That Haitian, she's a good one. She saves me. She doesn't have to save me like that, but she does," exclaims Emely.

This is not the first time Emely has shopped at Ana's colmado because she knows that Ana will not require her to find someone to vouch for her. And it is not the first time Emely has told me that Ana saves her and her family from hunger.

Like Emely, most residents of the Callejón and La Cienaga have been saved by intercultural fiao networks in corner stores. While other researchers have found that Haitians are categorically excluded from fiao in colmados, colmaderos in Cabarete recognize the benefits they accrue from both allowing others to vouch for Haitians and continuing to give in-store credit to Haitians who prove themselves as gente responsable. Everyday life in Cabarete, such as worshipping in the Haitian church, studying in the adult night school, and working in local places of employment, requires intercultural interaction between and among Dominicans, Haitians, and Dominico-Haitians, but borrower/creditor exchanges in corner stores is the only practice that creates a formal system of intercultural engagement in Cabarete. Anti-Haitian narratives are sometimes invoked in everyday engagement—whether at the church pulpit during a pastor's sermon or in a colmado when a shopkeeper discusses his fiao practices or between people at work—but just as often intercultural interactions are dependent upon working against these narratives. In the process of creating borrower/creditor exchanges in colmados, people appeal to other factors, such as people's shared position on the lowest rungs in the tourism industry, which consequently undermines long-standing explanations and expectations of Dominican-Haitian relations. Fiao in corner stores develops ties that bind people together in networks that they rely upon, especially in times of need.

Colmados have become a total social phenomenon in the Dominican Republic for their cultural, social, and economic benefits. Their ubiquity throughout the country evolved over time as a response to state investment in industrial agriculture, which led to deforestation and changing subsistence patterns for rural hunters, gatherers, and small-scale subsistence farmers, as well as increased urbanization. Becoming a shopkeeper grew to be a desirable employment opportunity, particularly for the opportunity to earn a permanent, year-round, less seasonally dependent income. Colmados, in both rural communities and urban neighborhoods, responded to the needs of the working class and poor people in a number of ways, most important of all was offering some people the chance to put their purchases on a tab to be paid each pay period or quincenal.

Most people shop in colmados, not only for their practical benefits, such as providing customers with the ability to purchase small amounts of staple foods, like small bags of prepared stewed beans or uncooked rice, which are cheaper and require less need for food storage, but also for the links between colmados and shopping for lo criollo, or homegrown food. For residents of the Callejón and La Cienaga, Janet's, the area's big-box supermarket, is frequented for a few of the services it provides, such as paying for cell phone service, but not for purchasing food. Shopping in supermarkets is viewed as foreign, lo extrajero, a way to purchase imported goods from other places, yet not goods from Haiti. Haitians complain that they are unable to find recognizable brands or goods for Haitian dishes, like black mushrooms, in area supermarkets. To compensate for this, one Haitian shopkeeper, Ana, travels to Haiti periodically and returns with Haitian goods for customers in Cabarete.

Many residents convey that colmados are good for the neighborhoods because the shops "keep their bellies full" in more ways than just food shopping. Colmados are central to Cabarete's foodscape for their role in not only the distribution and consumption of food but also for the flows of productive labor in and through these shops. Colmados hire local youth as ayudantes to assist customers with their purchases, recording in-store credit, and verifying orders made by distributors. Additionally, colmaderos allow local women to sell homemade prepared foods, such as bags of stewed beans and pastries like arepas and empanadas, in the mornings, a benefit for women who work outside the home and are unable to prepare the midday meal from scratch. They have come to rely on purchasing these prepared foods—a cheaper homegrown alternative to buying canned foods in the supermarket—to provide for their families. And colmados' delivery services are hired out to the area motorcycle taxi drivers, providing much-needed work for men who have migrated to the region from other places.

There are general social norms in colmados, such as colmaderos' usage of kin terms and terms of endearment based upon physical characteristics to greet customers, and colmaderos' uncanny way of knowing who to serve when as it is unlikely for customers to queue as they wait to for service. Moreover, there is a daily rhythm of food shopping in colmados; women shop in the mornings, looking for foodstuffs to prepare the midday meal and sometimes sending their children to shop in their stead, while men tend to shop during a work break or after work, sometimes frequenting a colmadón where they can engage in after-hours socializing with friends.

There are three different types of fiao: in-store credit to those who are known to be gente responsable, who request a gift without repaying the debt, and who are required to have someone vouch for them since they are unknown to the shopkeeper. These types are not differentiated in the notebook each colmado maintains to document in-store credit. Fiao is always recorded as a household, not individual, debt. Sometimes, colmaderos provide a gift of free food to people who request one. Residents who are looking for a gift typically seek out a colmado owned or staffed by a woman, acting on the presumption that women will provide certain ethics of care for others. But shopkeepers are astutely aware that the more gifts they give, the more risk they incur of falling into financial ruin. In other words, shopkeepers know that the financial solvency of their shops is dependent upon their customers' timely debt repayment. Offering fiao is a risk for shopkeepers, and an important part of their job is building the capacity to distinguish gente responsable from those who are not. Colmaderos allow customers to purchase food using in-store credit if the shopper is known as a person who typically repays their debts in a timely manner. However, in neighborhoods such as the Callejón and La Cienaga where almost everyone is underemployed in the tourist economy, it is difficult to ascertain who might be able to repay their debts on any given day. Borrower/creditor exchanges emerged to mitigate the risk of debt non-repayment to colmaderos.

The development of fiao as the primary method of payment in colmados has established morally charged discourses, or emergent moralities, of fiao in the Callejón and La Cienaga. Most residents use fiao routinely, and they report that repaying debt is part of their moral duty to being gente responsable. Furthermore, residents assert that allowing customers to make purchases using in-store credit is an important part of colmaderos' commitment to the moral good of the community. Some colmaderos refer to their faith in God or their moral compass when they discuss fiao. But not all residents perceive fiao in a positive light. In fact, there are a handful of upwardly mobile residents, all of whom attend the local Dominican Protestant church, who contend that fiao—both colmaderos' offering of it and customers' request of it—competes with individuals' duty to secure their own financial independence and security. In so doing, these residents argue that fiao should not be used, ignoring the real need of residents who, at many times of the year when tourism slows down, cannot make ends meet. Even during times of financial hardship, colmaderos and creditors report that there is relatively high debt repayment in the Callejón and La Cienaga—about 30% in each quincenal. Colmaderos and creditors have come to expect this rate of repayment; when borrowers repay at lower rates, they become known as irresponsible and are at risk of being denied fiao—not categorically, but temporarily until they provide evidence of repayment or higher, acceptable rates of repayment.

Borrower/creditor exchanges include a fair amount of hidden labor, making connections between those who lend and those who borrow simultaneously helpful and stressful. While colmaderos' fiao notebooks document how much people owe the shop, borrower/creditor exchanges require that people, not colmados, have to keep track of how much they have borrowed from and lent to whom when others vouch for them in the process of becoming gente responsable. Therefore, repaying these micro-debts includes the hidden labor of attending to relationships with people who have some financial well-being. The hidden labor of borrower/creditor exchanges also includes making multiple visits to borrowers to assure repayment. In fact, just a little over half of all borrower/creditor exchanges are made interculturally, meaning that Dominicans vouch for Haitians and Haitians vouch for Dominicans. Colmaderos and shoppers alike contend that these intercultural arrangements are beneficial to the well-being of colmados since it exposes shopkeepers to a wider array of people at any given time who might be responsible, allowing them to secure income and mitigate risk. In many borrower/creditor exchanges, women vouch for women and men vouch for men, but there are cases in which new heterosexual households form and people become gente responsable through these new household arrangements.

Colmados that are known as failing or struggling are called empty, meaning that they are empty of products on the shelves and of customers. The three most struggling or failing colmados are all owned by shopkeepers of Haitian descent, and two of these shopkeepers are Haitian women. Colmaderos who own struggling colmados are more apt, not less, to allow customers to use in-store credit to make purchases. Additionally, shopkeepers trying to keep failing colmados afloat often do not require borrowers to have someone vouch for them to use in-store credit. By all measures, borrowers repay debts to struggling colmados at a lower rate, and it is exactly this low repayment rate that colmaderos point to as the defining cause of their financial difficulties. While fiao can be a gift to borrowers in times of real need, overlending can severely cripple colmaderos and prevent them from repaying their own debts to distributors, creating a cycle of debt that is not easily overcome.

There are indeed times when people are unable to secure in-store credit, either directly from colmaderos or through creditors who agree to vouch for them. When this occurs, people regularly share food and meals, visiting people they know who might be able to spare some food or a whole meal to get them through until they are able to become gente responsable again. Food- and meal-sharing are very common, which highlights the fact that fiao is not attainable for everyone at all times. Unlike borrower/creditor exchanges, sharing food and meals is not intercultural but intracultural, and to avoid asking for too much, typically people share food with people who are not their creditors at that time.

My research in Cabarete calls into question some fundamental assumptions about life in Hispaniola that warrant further examination. Contrary to the logic of the fatal-conflict model that assumes strained, negative, or domineering Haitian-Dominican interpersonal relations, *Not Even a Grain of Rice* highlights the complexity of Dominican-Haitian relations. Results in Cabarete demonstrate the nuances of contemporary anti-Haitianism and its effects—or not—on interactions between and among Haitians and Dominicans. With surprising optimism, results show that people in Cabarete are working toward interpersonal and institutional social change. While there are residents in these neighborhoods who are actively countering anti-Haitianism and educating others to build much-needed understanding between people, intercultural borrower/creditor exchanges have arisen even when there has been little modification of people's anti-Haitian rhetoric. People demonstrate that they may hold distrusting views of the Other, but they often act in the Other's interest to widen their own social safety nets. Overall, intercultural engagement might indeed be determined by what Anna Tsing calls the "awkward, unequal, and unstable" in her understanding of friction. And while I agree with this characterization, *Not Even a Grain of Rice* emphasizes friction's "creative qualities of interconnection" unfolding as a social process within the context of Haitian-Dominican interactions in Cabarete.

Some residents in the Callejón and La Cienaga note that Haitians have a role in the tourist economy, particularly in international tourist destinations like Cabarete or Las Terrenas (on the Samaná peninsula) where more French-speaking tourists vacation. The fact that Haitians and Dominicans speak different languages, both of which are useful to local employers in the tourism industry, might decrease some of the stress between people and perhaps mitigate the stiff competition that could result as rivals in a scarce market economy. More research is needed to understand if alleviating competition, or even the perception of competition, in these job markets would have any effects on anti-Haitianism outside of these unique locales.

Not Even a Grain of Rice argues that for working-class residents of Cabarete, there is a tension between the moral discourse of care for others and the economic necessity of strategizing to preserve people's businesses and livelihoods. There is a strong economic incentive to offer fiao, creating moral discourses of intergroup solidarity. Shoppers, shopkeepers, and to a lesser extent, distributors traverse this tension by restraining racist beliefs and developing class solidarity and a shared sense of dignity through credit, even while asserting racist logics in other settings. Yet this complexity exists within a neoliberal political economy rooted in capturing international capital from tourism development which maintains high rates of under- and unemployment and the suppression of wages. Therefore, while fiao can be a helpful strategy for local residents to buy food and for shopkeepers and other laborers to maintain their businesses, in-store credit is not a sustainable, long-term strategy to curb poverty. Even with established borrower/creditor exchanges, customers and shopkeepers alike insist that they are still poor, just a few unpaid debts away from being cut off from using in-store credit and, in the case of shopkeepers, closing the doors of their colmados. Instead, a more beneficial and sustainable solution would be the ability to earn a living wage—an unrealistic prospect at this point because of the strictures of international capitalism.

It would be interesting to see if intercultural borrower/creditor exchanges like those found in colmados in Cabarete develop similarly in other multicultural international tourism destinations in the Dominican Republic, such as Punta Cana, the Samaná peninsula, or La Romana. Additionally, future research on colmados in communities with less daily intercultural engagement is needed to see if fiao is still categorically denied to Haitians, as it was in earlier studies of colmados in Santo Domingo (Murray 1996) and Santiago (Rosing 2009).

There have been recent calls for more research on Haitian-Dominican syncretism, such as ESENDOM's three-part series on "Research Ideas on Dominicans That You Should Pursue." The second installment of this series by Rodríguez and Santana (2018) proposes a project that seeks to highlight "the contradictions of Dominican society where racist anti-Haitian ideology prevails amid Haitian-Dominican collaboration and solidarity among ordinary people." The research idea suggests investigating topics such as the influence of the popular Haitian musical genre called kompa on Dominican merengue clásico through the work of Félix Cumbé, a Haitian artist who migrated to Dominican Republic at the age of thirteen. Heeds to this call for research on Haitian-Dominican collaboration, while not completely silent, have been slow. What is needed is more research on Haitian-Dominican relations in intercultural contexts, particularly in communities like Cabarete that are a distance from the border region and outside of bateys. At a time when the effects of La Sentencia can be felt throughout the hemisphere, it is important to fill the gap in our understanding of Haitian-Dominican relations. Furthermore, it is just as important to understand the intersections of identities, especially intersections of gender, class, and heritage, that affect people's experiences with successfully attaining fiao and borrower/creditor exchanges. While I in no way claim that there is no interpersonal discrimination against Haitians in the Dominican Republic, I offer up this ethnographic example in Cabarete to highlight the complexity of Dominican-Haitian relations, to show that everyday life in the Dominican Republic requires intercultural engagement and to give a more nuanced perspective on when and how discrimination is experienced in the Dominican Republic.

But *Not Even a Grain of Rice* also contributes to much broader conversations about identity formation, intercultural relations, and culture change in migrant-sending and migrant-hosting communities, particularly those communities at the center of international tourism. Residents in La Cienaga and the Callejón display compassion that is as practical as it is affective. Results in Cabarete show that differences do not impinge on people's capacity to create productive, helpful networks, especially when people creating the networks focus instead on characteristics that are all shared. But more cross-cultural research is needed with attention to intercultural relations in migrant-hosting communities when perceptions of the Other are influenced by transactional relations, such as fiao in Dominican Republic, and if these transactions lead to lasting, transformational culture change—changes that eliminate racism for good. In a world with millions of people on the move, with more information at our fingertips than ever before about how people live, it is hopeful to learn of practices that build solidarity. It remains to be seen if this class-based solidarity leads to any collective action calling for better working conditions for low-paid laborers regardless of citizenship. And if this collective action does materialize, it also remains to be seen whether or not it would have any impact on modifying structural economic relations that have perpetuated inequality and poverty in the region.

References

Adams, Abigail. 2019. "'Hard Work,' Forced Labor, and Q'eqchi' Maya Conversion to Evangelical Protestantism in Alta Verapaz, Guatemala." Paper presented on the panel, "'Hard Work' and 'Laziness' in Latin America: The Racial, Ethnic and Class Ideologies that Underpin Social Inequality." Latin American Studies Association, Boston, MA, 25 May.

Albee, Alana. 1996. "Banking for the Poor: Credit Mechanisms and Women's Empowerment." *Gender and Development* 4(3): 48–53.

Andújar, Carlos. 2004. *Identidad Cultural y Religiosidad Popular*. Santo Domingo: Editorial Letra Gráfica.

Appadurai, Arjun. 1996. *Modernity at Large: Cultural Dimensions of Globalization*. Minneapolis, MN: University of Minnesota Press.

———. 1990. "Disjuncture and Difference in the Global Cultural Economy." *Public Culture* 2(2): 1–24.

Aristy Escuder, Jaime. 1995. *Ahorro y producción de las microempresas y pequeñas empresas en la República Dominicana: un análisis econométrico, informe*. Santo Domingo: Fondo para el Financiamiento de la Microempresa, Inc.

Association of Black Anthropologists. 2014. "Statement on the DR Ruling." *Democracy and Justice in Haiti*. Accessed November 14, 2014. http://www.ijdh .org/2014/01/topics/immigration-topics/aba-statement-on-the-dominican-repub lic/.

Bishop, Marlon. 2019. *A Border Drawn in Blood*. Latino USA. María Hinojosa, Executive Producer. Accessed October 7, 2019. https://www.npr.org/sections /parallels/2017/10/07/555871670/80-years-on-dominicans-and-haitians-revisit-p ainful-memories-of-parsley-massacre?fbclid=IwAR1wiCd64DKZuglPJjKsUTD5i OPrr4_LUI8354SHtRAbExs2wpNfYr9IQEk.

Bishop, Marlon and Tatiana Fernandez. 2017. "80 Years On, Dominicans and Haitians Revisit Painful Memories of Parsley Massacre." Accessed October 7, 2019. https://www.npr.org/sections/parallels/2017/10/07/555871670/80-ye ars-on-dominicans-and-haitians-revisit-painful-memories-of-parsley massacre?

fbclid=IwAR1wiCd64DK ZuglPJjKsUTD5iOPrr4_LUI8354SHtRAbExs2wpN
fYr9IQEk.

Blalock, H. M. 1967. *Toward a Theory of Minority-Group Relations*. New York: John Wiley and Sons.

Blum, Lawrence. 2002. *"I'm Not a Racist, But:" The Moral Quandary of Race.* Ithaca, NY: Cornell University Press.

Bonilla-Silva, Eduardo. 2014. *Racism without Racists: Color-Blind Racism and the Persistence of Racial Inequality in America*. Fourth Edition. Lanham, MD: Rowman & Littlefield.

Brennan, Denise. 2004. *What's Love Got To Do With It? Transnational Desire and Sex Tourism in the Dominican Republic*. Durham: Duke University.

Candelario, Ginetta E. 2007. *Black Behind the Ears: Dominican Racial Identity from Museums to Beauty Shops*. Durham, NC: Duke University.

Carruyo, Light. 2008. *Producing Knowledge, Protecting Forests: Rural Encounters with Gender, Ecotourism, and International Aid in the Dominican Republic*. State College, PA: Pennsylvania State University.

Carvajal, Mayra. 2017. "Dominican Republic: Retail Foods. Diverse Retail Sector Facilitates Fifth-Largest Market for U.S. Consumer-Oriented Products in Latin America." USDA Foreign Agricultural Service. GAIN Report Number DR1718. Global Agricultural Information Network. Accessed September 9, 2019. https://ap ps.fas.usda.gov/newgainapi/api/report/downloadreportbyfilename?filename=Retail %20Foods_Santo%20Domingo_Dominican%20Republic_12-27-2017.pdf

Cohen, Deborah. 2013. *Braceros: Migrant Citizens and Transnational Subjects in the Postwar United States and Mexico*. University of North Carolina Press.

Corr, Rachel. 2016. "We Make Them Give More": Women's Roles in the Exchange and Redistribution of Food Across Ethnic Boundaries. *Food and Foodways* 24(3–4): 173–193.

Crenshaw, Kimberlé Williams. 1989. "Demarginalizing the Intersection of Race and Sex: A Black Feminist Critique of Antidiscrimination Doctrine, Feminist Theory and Antiracist Politics." *University of Chicago Legal Forum*, 139–167.

Derby, Lauren. 1998. "Chicken With Worms: Food and Nationalism in the Dominican Republic." In *Close Encounters of Empire: Writing the Cultural History of U.S.-Latin American Relations,* Gilbert M. Joseph, Catherin C. LeGrand, and Ricardo D. Salvatore, eds., pp. 457–488. Duke University Press.

———. 1994. "Haitians, Magic, and Money: Raza and Society in the Haitian-Dominican Borderlands, 1900 to 1937." *Comparative Studies in Society and History* 36(3): 488–526.

Deutsch, Tracey. 2001. "Untangling Alliances: Social Tensions Surrounding Independent Grocery Stores and the Rise of Mass Retailing." In *Food Nations: Selling Taste in Consumer Societies*, Warren Belasco and Philip Scranton, eds., pp. 156–174. New York: Routledge.

DeVault, Marjorie L. *Feeding the Family: The Social Organization of Caring as Gendered Work*. University of Chicago Press.

Di Giovine, Michael A. 2018. "Anthropologists Weigh In On Sustainability of Tourism." *Anthropology News* 58(4): 47–52.

Dominican Ministry of Tourism. 2019. "Dominican Republic Shares Record Breaking Tourism Numbers and Future Plans." Accessed September 13. https ://www.globenewswire.com/news-release/2019/03/29/1790123/0/en/Dominican -Republic-Shares-Record-Breaking-Tourism-Numbers-and-Future-Plans.html

Dominican Today. 2019. "Civic Group Demands a Fence Along Entire 388km Haiti Border." Accessed December 30. https://dominicantoday.com/dr/local/2019/12/20 /group-demands-a-fence-along-entire-388km-haiti-border/.

Elgin, John. 2020. "A Debate Over Identity and Race Asks, Are African-Americans 'Black' or 'black?'" *New York Times*, June 26. Accessed July 12. https://www.nyt imes.com/2020/06/26/us/black-african-american-style-debate.html.

Federación Nacional de Comerciantes Detallistas de Provisiones (FENACODEP). 2019. "Nosotros" y "Servicios." Accessed May 2018. http://fenacodep.org/.

Food and Agriculture Organization. 2016. "Food Security and Statistics (Dominican Republic)." www.fao.org/countryprofiles/index.asp?lang=en&paia=2&iso3=DOM.

García-Grandon, Daniela. 2019. "Moral Boundaries of Food Provisioning and Debt in Chile." Paper presented on the panel, "La desigualdad alimentaria en América Latina." Latin American Studies Association, Boston, MA, 26 May.

García-Peña, Lorgia. 2016. *The Borders of Dominicanidad: Race, Nation, and Archives of Contradiction*. Durham, NC: Duke University.

———. 2015. "Translating Blackness: Dominicans Negotiating Race and Belonging." *The Black Scholar* 45(2): 10–20.

Garth, Hanna. 2020. *Food in Cuba: The Pursuit of a Decent Meal*. Stanford, CA: Stanford University Press.

Geology.com. n.d. *Map of Caribbean*. Accessed July 5, 2016. geology.com/world/ca ribbean-satellite-image.shtml.

Gilligan, Carol. 2011. "Interview with Carol Gilligan." *Ethics of Care*. https://ethic-sofcare.org/carol-gilligan/.

Gilligan, Carol and Nel Noddings. 2009. "Care-Focused Feminism." In *Feminist Thought: A More Comprehensive Introduction*. Third Edition, Rosemarie Tong, ed. Boulder, CO: Westview Press.

Girard, William. 2019. "'Laziness' and 'Hard Work' and Other-than-Human Beings in Honduran Pentecostal Churches." Paper presented on the panel, "'Hard Work' and 'Laziness' in Latin America: The Racial, Ethnic and Class Ideologies that Underpin Social Inequality." Latin American Studies Association, Boston, MA, 25 May.

Graeber, David. 2012. *Debt: The First 5,000 Years*. New York: Melville House.

Grameen Bank. 2019. "Bank for the Poor: Grameen Bank." Accessed November 26. http://www.grameen.com/.

Gregory, Steven. 2014. *The Devil Behind the Mirror: Globalization and Politics in the Dominican Republic*. Second edition. Berkeley, CA: University of California.

Guzmán, Elena. 2019. "Checkpoint Nation." NACLA, March 22. Accessed August 1, 2019. https://nacla.org/news/2019/03/22/checkpoint-nation.

———. 2016. "Performing the Borders of Two Nations: Visual Representations of Haitian and Dominican Identity. "Paper presented at the annual meetings of the American Anthropological Association, Minneapolis, MN, 18 November.

Harvey, David. 2006. *Spaces of Global Capitalism: A Theory of Uneven Geographical Development.* New York & London: Routledge.

Hayes, Lauren A. 2017. "The Hidden Labor of Repayment: Women, Credit, and Strategies of Microenterprise in Northern Honduras." *Economic Anthropology* 4: 22–36.

Horn, Maja. 2014. "Dictates of Dominican Democracy: Conceptualizing Caribbean Political Modernity." *Small Axe: A Caribbean Journal of Criticism* 18(2): 18–35.

Howard, David. 2007. "Development, Racism, and Discrimination in the Dominican Republic." *Development in Practice* 17(6): 725–738.

International Mission Justice. 2015. "Commercial Sexual Exploitation of Children in the Dominican Republic." Accessed September 13. https://www.ijm.org/docum ents/studies/IJM-Commercial-Sexual-Exploitation-of-Children-in-the-Dominican -Republic.pdf.

Jayaram, Kiran. 2010. "Capital Changes: Haitian Migrants in Contemporary Dominican Republic." *Caribbean Quarterly* 56(3): 31–54.

Jefferson, Anna. 2013. "Narratives of Moral Order in Michigan's Foreclosure Crisis." *City and Society* 25(1): 92–112. doi: 10.1111/ciso.12006.

Jung, Yuson and Andrew Newman. 2014. "An Edible Moral Economy in the Motor City: Food Politics and Urban Governance in Detroit." *Gastroeconomica: Journal of Food and Culture* 14(1): 23–32.

Karim, Lamia. 2011. *Microfinance and Its Discontents: Women in Debt in Bangladesh.* Minneapolis, MN: University of Minnesota Press.

———. 2008. "De-Mystifying Micro-Credit: The Grameen Bank, NGOs and Neoliberalism in Bangladesh." *Cultural Dynamics* 20 (1): 5–29.

Keys, Hunter M, Bonnie N Kaiser, Jennifer W Foster, Rosa Y Burgos Minaya, and Brandon A Kohr. 2015. "Perceived Discrimination, Humiliation, and Mental Health: A Mixed-Methods Study of Haitian Migrants in the Dominican Republic." *Ethnicity and Health* 219–240.

Klein, Herbert S. 2011. *A Concise History of Bolivia.* Second Edition. Cambridge: Cambridge University Press.

Krohn-Hansen. 2016. "The Dominican Colmado from Santo Domingo to New York." In *Oxford Research Encyclopedia of Latin American History,* William Beezley, ed. New York: Oxford University Press.

———. 2013. *Making New York Dominican: Small Business, Politics, and Everyday Life.* Philadelphia, PA: University of Pennsylvania Press.

Lamb, Valerie and Lauren Dundes. 2017. "Not Haitian: Exploring the Roots of Dominican Identity." *Social Sciences* 6(132): 1–12.

Lappé, Frances Moore and Joseph Collins. 1977. Why Can't People Feed Themselves? In *Annual Editions: Anthropology 2008-09.* Thirtieth Edition, Elvio Angeloni, ed., pp. 165–169. Dubuque, IA: McGraw-Hill.

Leon, Ghislaine. 2015. "Meet Miss Rizos, The Woman Behind One of Santo Domingo's Only Natural Hair Salon." Remezcla, December 30. Accessed September 20, 2018.https://remezcla.com/features/culture/meet-miss-rizos-the-wo man-behind-santo-domingos-first-natural-hair-salon/.

Lopez, Gerald. "Moreno, Negro, Indio: Explained." La Galería: Voices of the Dominican Diaspora. Accessed, August 16, 2019. https://lagaleriamag.com/moren onegroindio/.

Low, Setha M. "Towards an Anthropological Theory of Space and Place." *Semiotica* 175(1/4): 21–37.

Lora, Janio (featuring Xiomara Fortuna). 2015. *Colmado*. Mi Nueva Edad.

Lozano, Wilfredo. 1997. "La urbanización de la pobreza." Santo Domingo.

Martínez, Samuel. 2007. *Decency and Excess: Global Aspiration and Material Deprivations on a Caribbean Sugar Plantation*. Routledge: New York.

———. 2003. "Not a Cockfight: Rethinking Haitian-Dominican Relations." *Latin American Perspectives* 30(3): 80–101.

———. 1999. "Hidden Hand to Heavy Hand: Sugar, the State, and Migrant Labor in Haiti and the Dominican Republic." *Latin American Research Review* 34(1): 57–84.

———. 1996. *Peripheral Migrants: Haitians and Dominican Republic Sugar Plantations*. University of Tennessee.

Mateo, Lucirys. 2017. *Identidad, diversidad cultural, y migración: Grupo étnico del Pequeño Haiti, Barrio San Carlos*. Asesor: Luciano Castillo Domínguez. Tésis en la Facultad de Humanidades, Escuela de Historia y Antropología, Universidad Autónoma de Santo Domingo. Santo Domingo, Dominican Republic.

Mauss, Marcel. [1950]1990. *The Gift: Forms and Functions of Exchange in Archaic Societies*. Translated by W. D. Halls. London: Routledge Press.

Mayol, Virgilio. 2019. "Dominican Republic: Food Processing Ingredients, 2019." USDA Foreign Agricultural Service. Global Agricultural Information Network. GAIN Report Number DR1902. Accessed January 9, 2019. https://apps.fas.usda.gov/newgainapi/api/report/downloadreportbyfilename?filename=Food%20Processing%20Ingredients_Santo%20Domingo_Dominican%20Republic_3-19-2019.pdf.

Miles, Ann. *From Cuenca to Queens: An Anthropological Story of Transnational Migration*. Austin, TX: University of Texas.

Miller, Daniel. 2001. *The Dialectics of Shopping*. Chicago: University of Chicago Press.

Minority Rights Group International. 2018. "World Directory of Minorities and Indigenous Peoples - Dominican Republic: Haitians." Accessed July 31, 2019. https://www.refworld.org/docid/49749d2e21.html.

Moya Pons, Frank. 2011. "La Cuestión Haitiana." *Diario Libre*, May 14. Accessed January 12, 20. www.diario.libre.com/noticias_det.php?id=290423.

———. 1998. *Dominican Republic: A National History*. Princeton: Markus Weiner Press.

Mpogole, H, I Mwaungulu, S. Mlasu, and G. Lubawa. 2012. "Multiple Borrowing and Loan Repayment: A Study of Microfinance Clinents at Iringa, Tanzania." *Global Journal of Management and Business Research* 12(4): 97–101.

Murray, George. 1996. *El Colmado: Una Exploración Antropológica del Negocio de Comidas y Bebidas en la República Dominicana*. Santo Domingo: Fondo para el Financiamiento de la Microempresa, Inc.

Nations Online. 2016. *Map of Dominican Republic*. July 5. www.nationsonline.org/oneworld/map/dominican-republic-map.htm.

Nealon, Jeffrey. 2012. *Post-postmodernism: or, the Cultural Logic of 'Just-in-Time' Capitalism*. Palo Alto, CA: Stanford University Press.

O'Dougherty, Maureen. 2002. *Consumption Intensified: The Politics of Middle-Class Daily Life in Brazil*. Raleigh, NC: Duke University Press.

Oficina Nacional de Estadísticas. 2016. "Tu Municipio en Cifras." Accessed April 7, 2017. www.one.gov.do/categoria/TuMunicipioEnCifras.

Ortner, Sherry. 2003. *New Jersey Dreaming: Capital, Culture, and the Class of '58*. Raleigh, NC: Duke University Press.

Paley, Julia. 2001. *Marketing Democracy: Power and Social Movements in Post-Dictatorship Chile*. University of California Press.

Pan American Health Organization. 2017. Health in the Americas: "Dominican Republic" and "Haiti." Accessed October 24, 2019. https://www.paho.org/salud-en-las-americas-2017/?p=4110.

Peebles, Gustav. 2010. "The Anthropology of Credit and Debt." *Annual Review of Anthropology* 39: 225–240.

Petrozziello, Allison J. (with Amelia Hintzen and Juan Carlos González Díaz). 2014. *Género y el Riesgo de Apatridia para la Población de Ascendencia Haitiana de los Bateyes de la República Dominicana*. Centro para la Observación Migratoria y el Desarrollo en el Caribe, Santo Domingo: Editorial Búho.

Petrozziello, Allison J. and Bridget Wooding. 2012. *Fanm Nan Fwontye, Fanm Toupatou: Making Visible the Violence Agtainst Haitian Migrant, In-transit and Displaced Women on the Dominican-Haitian Border*. Santo Domingo: Observatory Migrants of the Caribbean (OBMICA).

Pintor, José Enrique. 2007. *Sanky Panky*. Coral Films.

Poe, Tracy N. 1999. "The Origins of Soul Food in Black Urban Identity: Chicago, 1915–1947." *American Studies International* 37 (1): 4–33.

Portes, Alejandro and Rúben G. Rumbaut. 2001. *Legacies: The Story of the Immigrant Second Generation*. University of California Press.

Rahier, Jean Muteba. 2003. Introduction: *Mestizaje, Mulataje, Mestiçagem* in Latin American Ideologies of National Identities. *Journal of Latin American Anthropology* 8(1): 40–50.

Regalado, Pedro A. 2016. "Bodegas and Colmados: Dominican Vernacular Space in Washington Heights." The Gotham Center of New York History. Accessed August 10, 2018. https://www.gothamcenter.org/blog/bodegas-and-colmados-dominican-vernacular-space-in-washington-heights.

Ricourt, Milagros. 2016. *The Dominican racial Imaginary: Surveying the Landscape of Race and Nation in Hispaniola*. New Brunswick, NJ: Rutgers University.

Riveros, Natalia. 2014. *Estado de la Cuestión de la Población de los Bateyes Dominicanos en Relación a la Documentación*. Centro para la Observación Migratoria y el Desarrollo en el Caribe, Santo Domingo: Editorial Búho.

Rodríguez, Amaura and Nelson Santana. 2018. "Fifteen Research Ideas on Dominicans That You Should Pursue (Part 2)." *ESENDOM: Cultura y Conciencia*. 27 March. Accessed August 29, 2019.

Rodríguez Grullón, Altair. 2013. *Estado del Arte de las Migraciones que Atañen a la República Dominicana*. Centro para la Observación Migratoria y el Desarrollo en el Caribe, Santo Domingo: Editorial Búho.

Roitman, Janet. 2005. *Fiscal Disobedience: An Anthropology of Economic Regulation in Central Africa.* Princeton, NJ: Princeton University Press.

Rosing, Howard. 2009. "Economic Restructuring and Urban Food Access in the Dominican Republic." *National Association for the Practice of Anthropology (NAPA) Bulletin* 32 (1): 55–76.

———. 2007. *La Comida Vacia: Neoliberal Resturcturing and Urban Food Access in the Dominican Republic (unpublished dissertation).* Binghamton: State University of New York.

Ross, Andrew. 2013. *Creditocracy and the Case for Debt Refusal.* New York: OR Books.

Salario Mínimo. 2019. "Salario Mínimo en la República Dominicana." Accessed October 24. https://salariominimo.info/republica-dominicana/.

Sanabria, Harry. 2007. *The Anthropology of Latin America and the Caribbean.* London: Pearson.

Santana, Ricardo. 2015. "Matan a un haitiano y cuelgan su cadaver en un parque en Santiago." *Listín Diario*. February 12. Accessed May 6, 2015. http://www.listindia rio.com/la-republica/2015/2/11/355855/Matan-a-un-haitiano-y-cuelgan-su-cada ver-en-un-parque-en-Santiago.

Schafer, Daniel L. 2013. *Zephaniah Kinsley Jr and the Atlantic World: Slave Trader, Plantation Owner, Emancipator.* Gainesville: University Press Florida.

Schuller, Mark. 2012. *Killing with Kindess: Haiti, International Aid, and NGOs.* New Brunswick: Rutgers.

Schneider, David M. 1980. *American Kinship: A Cultural Account.* University of Chicago Press.

Shakow, Miriam. 2019. "Who is 'Working Hard' in Evo's Bolivia? Debates among a new Middle Class, 1995–2019." Paper presented on the panel, "'Hard Work' and 'Laziness' in Latin America: The Racial, Ethnic and Class Ideologies that Underpin Social Inequality." Latin American Studies Association, Boston, MA, 25 May.

Simmons, Kimberly Eison. 2009. *Reconstructing Racial Identity and the African Past in the Dominican Republic.* Gainesville, FL: University Press of Florida.

———. 2008. "Navigating the Racial Terrain: Blackness and Mixedness in the United States and the Dominican Republic." *Transforming Anthropology* 16(2): 95–111.

Sittig, Ann L., and Martha Florinda González. 2016. *The Mayans Among Us: Migrant Women and Meatpacking on the Great Plains.* Lincoln, NE: Bison Books/ University of Nebraska.

Sobzak, Michael. 2010. *The New Americans: Recent Immigration and American Society: American Attitudes toward Immigrants and Immigration Policy.* El Paso, TX: LFB Scholarly Publishing.

Smith, Betty. 2001 [1943]. *A Tree Grows in Brooklyn.* New York: Harper Perennial.

Smith, Valene L. 1989. *Hosts and Guests: The Anthropology of Tourism.* Philadelphia, PA: University of Pennsylvania Press.

Stout, Noelle. 2016. "#INDEBTED: Disciplining the Moral Valence of Mortgage Debt Online." *Cultural Anthropology* 31(1): 82–106.

Thornton, Brendan Jamal and Diego Ubiera. 2019. "Caribbean Exceptions: The Problem of Race and Nation in Dominican Studies." *Latin American Research Review* 54(2): 413–428.

Thorp, Rosemary. 2012. "A Historical Perspective on the Political Economy of Inequality in Latin America." In *The Oxford Handbook of Latin American Political Economy*, Javier and Jeff Dayton-Johnson Santiso, eds., pp. 149–168. Oxford University Press.

Torres-Saillant, Silvio. 2000. "The Tribulation of Blackness: Stages of Dominican Racial Identity." *Callaloo* 23(3): 1086–1111.

Tsing, Anna Lowenhaupt. 2005. *Friction: An Ethnography of Global Connection.* Princeton University Press.

United Nations Economic and Social Council. 2008. "Implementation of the International Covenant on Economic, Social, and Cultural Rights: Dominican Republic." Third periodic reports submitted by States parties under articles 16 and 17 of the Covenant. Substantive session of 2010.

Van Vleet, Krista E. 2019. Comments on "'Hard Work' and 'Laziness' in Latin America: The Racial, Ethnic and Class Ideologies that Underpin Social Inequality." Latin American Studies Association, Boston, MA, 25 May.

Whitten, Norman E., and Arlene Torres. 1998. *Blackness in Latin America and the Caribbean.* Vols. 1 and 2. Bloomington, IN: Indiana University Press.

World Food Programme. 2017. WFP Strategic Plan: 2017–2021. Accessed May 20, 2018. https://docs.wfp.org/api/documents/WFP0000019573/download/?_ga=2.58513514.1756278987.1578673633-1040449418.1578673633.

Wynne, Kimberly. 2014. "Dominican and Haitian Neighbors: Making Moral Attitudes and Working Relationships in the Banana Bateys." *Iberoamericana: Nordic Journal of Latin American and Caribbean Studies* XLIV (1–2): 149–172.

Zigon, Jarrett and C. Jason Throop. 2014. "Moral Experience: Introduction." *Ethos* 42(1): 1–15.

Zigon, Jarrett. 2007. "Moral Breakdown and the Ethical Demand: A Theoretical Framework for an Anthropology of Moralities." *Anthropological Theory* 7(2): 131–150.

Index

Note: *Italicized* pages refer to figures/tables.

149

About the Author

Christine Hippert, PhD/MPH, is professor of anthropology in the Department of Archaeology and Anthropology at the University of Wisconsin–La Crosse, where she has been on the faculty since 2007. She teaches courses on the anthropology of food, medical anthropology, culture change, social/economic/racial justice, and Latin American and Caribbean studies. As a cultural anthropologist with a graduate degree in public health, she has conducted long-term ethnographic research for over twenty years throughout Latin America and the Caribbean, primarily in the Dominican Republic, Bolivia, and Mexico. Christine has also conducted applied anthropological research in the United States, including leading a collaborative team of public health practitioners and undergraduate students in an evaluation of the Farm 2 School program in the school district of La Crosse, Wisconsin. Her research examines people's experiences of community development, health care, and food security as they relate to social constructions and the cultural politics of racial, ethnic, gendered, and national identities. The results of her research have been published in interdisciplinary journals such as *Food and Foodways*, *The Journal of Latin America and Caribbean Anthropology*, *Women's Studies International Forum*, *Bolivian Research Review*, *Practicing Anthropology*, and *Wadabagei: The Journal of the Caribbean and Its Global Diaspora*. Christine is former president and an active member of the North Central Council of Latin Americanists (NCCLA), a professional organization of scholars of Latin American and Caribbean Studies in the Midwest that fosters community outreach and education on topics related to Latin America and the Caribbean.

CPSIA information can be obtained
at www.ICGtesting.com
Printed in the USA
LVHW080750290822
726885LV00012B/332